# YOU AND CHANGE

## How to deal with Change

by

## Margo Kirtikar Ph.D

ISBN: 1-4033-4439-6 (E-book)
ISBN: 1-4033-4440-X (Paperback)

This book is printed on acid free paper.

© 1995 1$^{st}$ edition
Cover Design by Margo

1st Books - rev. 01/02/03

for all
those
who want to
live through change
effectively

# Table of Contents

# Preface

You and Change is on how to handle yourself and your life in times of chaos and change. Coping with our lives and our relationships with the people in our world depends on how successful we are in managing ourselves. It is through self-reflection, self-knowledge and self-acceptance that we are able to manage ourselves. How open we are to communicate with the world depends on how much we like ourselves, how much we understand ourselves and how motivated we are. We are all subject to an inner impulse to develop towards higher consciousness and the extent to which we resist this process is up to each one of us. We are all interconnected and each of us is a part of the WHOLE. We are all, regardless of our race or background, in the same boat and on the same journey. For those who are searching and those who disbelieve in the metaphysical, this book is a good practical beginning on the path of remembrance. As Erich Fromm says: *'For the first time in history the physical survival of the human race depends on a radical change of the human heart.'*

Change is not only an external cause that befalls us; we harbor change like a vessel. We are the recipients as well as the motor of change. You are the process and change all at once. Although this book is conceived for newcomers to this subject, I have tried to pay heed to the complex aspects of change. Accordingly, parts of the book are composed as investigation, others as exegesis and yet other parts as a practical handbook on how to refine our human powers as actors and recipients of change.

Alvin Toffler, in Future Shock says: *'We are creating a new society. Not a changed society. Not an extended, larger-than-life version of our present society. But a new society. Unless we understand this, we shall destroy ourselves in trying to cope with tomorrow. What is occurring now is not a crisis of capitalism, but of industrial society itself, regardless of its political form. We are simultaneously experiencing a youth revolution, a sexual revolution, a racial revolution, a colonial revolution, an economic revolution, and the most rapid and deep-going technological revolution in history. In a word, we are in the midst of the super-industrial revolution.'*

We are also experiencing a revolution of the individual. 'The universe is sometimes called the big man and man is sometimes known as the small universe.' This book has been written with a deep enthusiasm for the changes we are currently undergoing and with a strong belief in the power of each individual to contribute to the game between 'The Big Man' and 'The Small Universe.'

# A Note to the Reader

Much has changed in our world since the first edition of 'You and Change' was published over six years ago. Wars, accidents due to human error or negligence and natural disasters have caused horrific damage, death and suffering worldwide, but none had the same effect on the world as the formidable sudden attack in the US in September 2001, that killed over 4000 multi national innocent civilians. I believe that in this moment as people watched the planes crashing into the World Trade Center in shock, horror and disbelief there was an instant global recognition that our world and the life we have so far known has now changed forever. Collectively we realized that we have entered a new era of our world history and like it or not we are now forced to think differently, forced to view our world with different eyes and forced to re-evaluate our motives and actions.

The rules of the game of life of world economics, global environment, political and social have changed and in order for us to operate in this new world that we do not as yet fully grasp, we have no other choice but to expand in our awareness and understanding.

Many today are on a search path looking for guidance in religion or esoteric alternatives. Paralyzed, motivated or driven by fear some become fanatics and others become reckless. Fear has taken over and is in the very air we breathe. Fear of dying, of losing loved ones, losing wealth or savings, homes or jobs. This is not surprising, as we are living in a perplexed and contradictory world. Old world versus new world, old thinking versus new thinking, closed minds versus open minds, hate versus compassion, ignorance versus intelligence, and most recently a war of civilizations. Our freedom that we, the more privileged, have taken for granted is now being threatened. More than ever now we need to be emotionally stable and mentally aware to cope with this new danger.

The key to survive through this chaos is to acquire the ability to become both independent and interdependent. We need to think independently, to take responsibility individually for our thoughts and actions and at the same time we need to think collectively and understand that we are all inter related and therefore inter-dependent. We are all in this together, regardless of race, color, belief and gender. No one religion can claim the one and only truth, no one philosophy can claim to have all knowledge, no one people can claim superiority. There is today no excuse for ignorance and narrow mindedness. We live today in a world that offers enough living cultural alternatives that leaves no room for ignorance, hate, racism or separatism of any kind. Knowledge is available for anyone who seeks it and is willing to think. It is up to us individually to make the effort. Together we can all make a difference. It is the responsibility of the strong to help the weak, the wealthy to help the poor and those who have knowledge to teach those who are eager to learn. It is up to us individually to change things for the better by caring and sharing natural resources and to put a stop on every level to selfishness, ignorance, corruption, greed and to the spread of fanatism.

Few are aware that the power to change our life and our world for the better is in our hands. The change needs to occur first within the psyche of each one of us individually. The prerequisite for the inner change is to purify the self of all negative energies. As we eliminate the negative from our thoughts and emotions we automatically improve the quality of our life and that of our immediate environment. This will send a ripple effect spreading out to the atmosphere of our environment and that of our globe. Everything great that was ever achieved started out with little steps. This book 'You and Change' is meant to be a guide to show you simple and practical steps to self-discovery and self-transformation to a higher level of awareness. In order to connect with the Divine within, we need first to know and understand ourselves. My book 'Visions Unusual' is an introduction to the immaterial world, our inter-relationship with the cosmos and our individual spirituality. Once we understand and experience our own spirituality, connect to the cosmic energies and the Source, we begin to see the world with different eyes and life will begin to have meaning for us. Without this connection life is meaningless.

Margo.

October 2001

# To the Reader,

I have had to deal with endless conflicts and changes in my life like so many of us. Had I not developed the ability to analyze and to reflect, to sort out and soak in the good, to discard with awareness the bad and undesired, adapt and re-adapt, in a continuous state of transformation, I would have ended up a bundle of total confusion. In short a complete mess ripe for the loony bin.

This desire to understand my world and this urge to survive without losing my identity or forgetting who I am came from deep within me. At a very young age I discovered this 'well' of endless power and strength, in my most inner self, that was always there. I had great respect for this source which I intuitively felt was far mightier than myself, which never let me down, even in my most painful moments, helping me to emerge bigger and stronger than before after every ordeal. I am always aware of this Higher Power as a very important part of my life guiding me and protecting me. Circumstances in my life have led me having to spend a lot of time alone and yet I have seldom experienced the feeling of loneliness. For me this Higher Power was my Guardian Angel. Later I learned that it is also called the Higher Self. What we call it makes no difference as long as we are aware of its presence, acknowledge, respect it and love it. Each one of us, without exception is accompanied by a Higher Self or Guardian Angel throughout our lives.

With this book I would like to give you some helpful hints on how to handle yourself and your life in times of change and crisis. How to find contact with your inner self, and a universal reservoir of energy, strength and peace. Your store of infinite intelligence and wisdom. This book is meant to guide everyone who is genuinely open minded and willing to make the effort towards self-realization. For those who might not really know how or where to begin and also to inspire the intellects and those who are not quite ready yet to accept the idea of growth and self-transformation as the ultimate goal in life. Truth is always crystal clear and very simple. I present the guidelines in this book to lead you toward self-transformation as clearly and as simply as possible.

Margo

1995

*Change is an inevitable part of our lives*
*and yet many refuse to accept this.*
*Many of us fight change stubbornly,*
*making life miserable for ourselves and*
*for others around us,*
*both privately and professionally.*

*We have the power to change that!*
*We have the power*
*to create a better world for ourselves!*

# 1

# Change is Inevitable

Change is Inevitable
Change is the way of life
Change is necessary and
change is always difficult.

Or is it?
Yes and No.

It is true
Sometimes it is more difficult
Other times it is less difficult
It all depends on how you look at it.

Some manage change easily
Some manage change badly
Why?

Look at it this way –
At birth
You are given a role to play
And your stage is set for you.
This is a fact that you cannot change.

But from then on, it is up to you.
Some are born with much and go nowhere
Others are born with nothing and go far
materially, mentally or spiritually.

This proves one point.
Where you start from is unimportant.*
What really matters is
where you go from there.
Where you go,
and how you get there,
depends entirely on you.

You are responsible for your life
and what you do with it.
You are responsible for your thoughts
You are responsible for your actions.
This includes how you handle change.

You cannot escape change,
it is a part of life,
for all of us alike.

Life is motion and all is change.
Nothing moves forward and
nothing grows without the process of
change.

Good times change to bad times and
bad times change to good times.

Change is a cycle of life.
It is in constant motion,
neither you nor I can stop this.

You cannot hold on to time
Keeping it at a status quo.
As little as you can hold on to water
in the palm of your hand.

You cannot turn back the clock!

You cannot hold on to a moment of joy.
What you can do is live in the moment
And hold the memory fresh forever in
your mind.
Some people make a habit
of holding on to sorrow and pain,
forever blocking themselves,
both from living the moment and
from moving forward.

Holding on to old ways of thinking,
willing nothing to change,
is fighting a losing battle.

There is no guarantee in life and
security is an illusion.

We are all creative beings
and intelligent by nature.
Intelligence is our birthright.

Contact with our intuition,
contact with a Higher Power
gives us inner strength,
courage, power and love.
It gives us the power
to work miracles in our lives.

Power to be who we are.
Power to be true to ourselves and
power to cope with change.

Inner peace and wisdom
is earned through experiencing change.

Intuition and intelligence
is there for all alike,
waiting to be tapped by each and
everyone.
It is there to serve us
waiting at our beckoned call.

Love and joy are the great motors of life.
With love for ourselves and all around us
and with joy in our heart for life,
we are able to overcome all hardships in
our lives,
all pain and suffering become bearable.
Any change becomes bearable.

Change presents you with challenges.
Change offers you new opportunities,
giving you a chance to mend your ways.
Change gives you insight into yourself,
giving you a chance to expand and grow.

The decision is yours to take.

It is up to you to face change
and it is up to you to accept the challenge.
It is up to you to stand straight
and to discover the way through change,
to a much stronger and livelier YOU.

*I am obviously referring here only to people born within an acceptable social setting. Not to children born into hopeless distressful situations where there is absolutely no hope for them.

Buddha said:

> *'Everything arises and passes away,*
> *When you see this, you are above*
> *sorrow. This is the shining way.'*

# 2

# The Law of Change

In everything and everyone the law of growth is through eternal change. Change is the tool of human progress and it is through the law of change that the human race has moved from the animal family and has evolved into a higher intelligence. No living thing or situation is the same two minutes in succession. We can look around us and everything we see is subject to change, everything in nature is either growing or deteriorating. Nothing remains the same forever, whatever the cause is, natural catastrophes or technology, in time everything we know changes, as we are. Our relationship to our families, friends, neighbors and work associates are all subject to the same law of Change. Wars, epidemics or diseases and other irresistible forces of nature, force us to free ourselves of old habits and stagnation and to start all over again. The nation, business or industry, which neglects to keep moving forward through change, is ultimately doomed to fail. It is no different with individuals. Refusing to understand and to adapt to this law of change is the major cause of misfortunes and defeats.

Rapid changing circumstances demand that we readjust our outlook, our expectations and values. We find it very difficult to let go of all that we cherish, even though that which we cherish sometimes brings us frustration and resignation. We hang on stubbornly, refusing to acknowledge the new, the unfamiliar, we hold on to our old habitual thoughts and behavior patterns and our life becomes an endless state of hardship, struggle and failure.

Major discoveries in science and technology are being made every day, taking giant leaps forward unfathomable to the average person. We all, therefore, owe it to ourselves to keep ourselves informed, to educate ourselves and not only to understand but also to accept and to act accordingly. We owe it, just as much to our children, our families; our friends and business associates and we owe to society that we accept these changes so that we can contribute our share to life constructively.

The law of change is the greatest source of education. Once you can accept this, you will no longer oppose the changes which are forced upon you through private, professional, global or natural catastrophes which are beyond your control. Besides, on a practical level, it might help to keep in mind that flexibility of personality and the capacity of the individual to adapt to all circumstances, is one of the major factors of an attractive dynamic personality.

It requires effort to keep up with change. It calls for will power, determination and persistence. There is also a certain amount of suffering involved, which is an inevitable part of the transformation process. Pain and suffering serve to tear down the guards and barriers that you have built up to protect yourself, forcing you to meet your most inner self, allowing you to learn who you really are. It takes courage to step out of self-imposed limitations and to face oneself. It also requires an open mind, patience and flexibility to recognize the many opportunities that life is continuously offering you. No transformation is possible unless you can face and accept your inner true self with all your weaknesses and your strengths.

Hazel Henderson from The Politics of the Solar Age has the following to say: ' *If we can recognize that change and uncertainty are basic principles, we can greet the future and the transformation we are undergoing with the understanding that we do not know enough to be pessimistic. The life force within each of us can then* focus on the possible and the potentialities. One can call it faith in the future, or the acknowledgement that we are not in charge and that the planet is not a spaceship that we humans are 'steering' or 'managing.' This old fashioned image has served its purpose, but it encouraged our childish fascination with vehicles, transportation, speed and power. The maturing understanding, growing by age-old religious and mythic traditions, is that we are a conscious part of the earth — no mechanical spaceship, but a living planet, a total, teeming, pulsating, living organism: Gaia, the mysterious, self-organizing Earth Mother, nurturer of us — and all life.'

And Mary Bailey simply says: 'Increasingly, as we look to the future and compare what we hope for humanity with what appears to be the state of the world today, we realize how much depends upon the attitude and the actions of each and everyone of us.'

Transformation on the outside is the result of transformation on the inside. The focus is on individual inner transformation.

**3**

# Personal Change

No two minutes in a row are you the same. Your physical body is undergoing changes all the time. Every cell in your body is constantly in action, even while you are asleep. Your skin, your organs, your hair, your nails, your whole body is changing renewing itself in a continuous process. Every minute there is a new physical you and you are growing and changing constantly. It is a process that began from the instant you were conceived and will only stop with your death.

Imagine your body as a miraculous machine that came to life at your birth, plugged in for energy to the universal source through your breath, and this machine never ever stops. Certain parts of the body have always to be functioning in order for the body to continue to live. Even while you sleep, your body, the machine is still in full operation though on a lower energy level. While you are resting the body is regenerating and recharging itself from the universal battery. You are still breathing, your organs are still functioning, your stomach is digesting your dinner, your lungs are still pumping the breath of life into your system through your nose and your skin and your blood is circulating, all to keep you alive while you are resting. While you sleep your hearing remains active. Although your physical eyes are closed and resting your inner vision is switched on and you experience your dreams. This means that your brain your thinking machine, and your psyche are active busy digesting all that you have experienced physically, emotionally and mentally during your waking hours. Your body is even by nature preprogrammed to produce the necessary chemicals needed to renew and to heal itself. Stop here for one minute and ponder on that. Reflect on the miracle of your body, this perfect machine, preprogrammed to grow and to change. Reflect on the fact that your body is given to you in trust for no other reason than to serve you, it is all yours to do with as you please, to handle with care, to develop or to abuse. You have the freedom of choice; you are the master of your physical body.

As you are growing, you are also continuously living the process of learning. As a baby you automatically, instinctively, pick up everything and anything that happens around you. You register every sound, every smell, every color, every touch and every word around you. You mimic and copy grownups like a monkey, and then you begin to walk and talk. You are in the process of being programmed from the day you are born and you are continuously, consciously or subconsciously, storing information, thoughts, feelings and habits, all of which will influence your behavior and outlook on life as you grow older. You do all this automatically according to your own perceptions and abilities.

Then you go to school and you learn to adapt to new and unfamiliar environments. You pick up more data, expanding your reservoir of memories and experiences. You make new friends, learn new languages and later more intricate subjects. You play sports and learn to use your body in different ways. You expand mentally, physically and emotionally. You enter the adult world and you are constantly busy learning, growing and adapting, all of which is a natural process with a strong formative influence to which you generally respond without much thought or extra effort. You would assume, therefore, that by now being so accustomed to the process of change, you would have no problem dealing with it at any time and in whatever form. You could imagine that as you get older, it would be just as natural for you to learn and to adapt automatically each time, as easily as when you were a child.

The reality, however, is different. As we reach adulthood we are already quite conditioned physically, emotionally and mentally, with the experiences and sensations from our past environment, parents, family, relatives, school, teachers and friends. And if we have been taking in and accepting absolutely everything the desirable and the less desirable that we have been exposed to, then it can happen that some of our software, in certain areas of our brain computer, is already quite full or perhaps even totally blocked. The stage at which we become less and less receptive to new ideas and information, emotionally, intellectually or physically varies with each individual.

Our perception and reactions to new environments and experiences, as we grow older, differ and we each have our particular ways of dealing with change, depending on the data received in our younger age. For example, if we grew up with parents who themselves were fearful and insecure then we might be the same and repeat the same pattern. We tend to pick up habits and to copy people who influence us. We pick up thoughts, behavior, values, beliefs, both the good and the bad automatically, as we perceive them and store them in our memory bank. If we have been abused and hurt badly as children, we might develop a personal defense mechanism and we block our feelings to protect ourselves, jamming our emotional circuits. If at any time someone comes along using the same words, gestures or has a particular look or a smell that reminds us of our old hurt, our internal red lights start blinking and our heart beats faster, warning us instantly of danger and hurt. Our invisible defense walls immediately go up, we become totally closed and tense. We are then blind to reality, incapable of rational or intelligent thought. If we have been terribly hurt by a loved one, some of us are unable to fall in love again. We keep the feeling of pain alive in us as protection, completely overpowering any feeling of warmth, joy or love making us emotionally crippled, blocked to have an intimate and loving relationship ever again.

When you are young and you are dependent on your parents, you have very little choice in changing your environment. Generally, however, as a teenager, you begin to make choices, you choose your friends, fields of interest in study and leisure. You begin to find out more about yourself, what you like and what you dislike. Your own choices become more precise as you move on and join the world of adults. Then you become a professional, perhaps get married and have children. You take on more commitments and responsibilities, and you continue dealing with your life the best way you know how. As long as your life is running smoothly, without any major mishaps or calamities and develops in accordance with your plans to meet all your desired goals, you are happy. You have no problem with the changes you experience as long as circumstances in your life change for the better and everything is going your way. That is obviously easy and pleasant and you find that life is just a bowl of cherries. It is only when things take a bad turn and you begin to meet obstacles in your life, as we all inevitably do, that you are being put to the real test in life. It is during times of trouble that you discover your true character. You might be able to rise up to the situation and take charge adapting to the new situation. Very often you surprise yourself and you discover new qualities in yourself which you were so far unaware of. On the other hand, you might have a big problem, and you find yourself, for whatever reason, unable to deal with the obstacles that life is presenting to you. At such times, when you have difficulties to deal with changes in your life, it means, you are being given a signal, that this is a new situation which is interfering with your old programming. Some previous experience is blocking you from accepting this change. As a result you are confused, frightened and at a loss as to how to handle the problem.

At this point there are only two alternatives. The first would be that you fall apart completely. You lose control, shift the blame on some other person dumping the responsibility in their lap, or you hide behind an illness or perhaps conveniently have an accident. The second would be that you take control. You take matters into your own hands, accept the circumstances as they are and quickly readjust your thoughts and behavior as good as you possibly can, you roll up your sleeves, you take charge of the situation, you cooperate with the inevitable, in other words stand up to the test. By seeing the challenge in the face, having courage and taking the latter course, you overcome the old hurt automatically canceling the old program as you replace it with a new pattern of behavior. Whatever you decide to do or not do will not only have a ripple effect on everyone around you, but also you will have already begun to shape your own destiny.

*'God, give me the courage
to change the things I can change
and the strength to accept
the things I cannot change,
and the wisdom to be able
to tell one from the other.'*
*Prayer*

# 4

# **The Phases of Change**

Change in your life has many facets. Change can occur in your life without you even noticing it. It can creep up slowly on you giving you ample time to go through the process of readjusting. It can also hit you hard like an ice cold shower when you least expect it and catch you totally unprepared. Some changes in your life are welcome and other changes not at all. Perhaps you are someone who takes matters into your own hands and change your circumstances any time you feel it necessary to do so. One thing is sure, either way change will alter you, your life style and your relationships.

If you can adopt an attitude of accepting and quickly adjusting, you will no doubt be a happier person, gaining tremendous strength and courage, and you will not only be enriching your own life but also everybody's life around you. Change in your life can happen in three different ways; personal inner transformation in your character, economic changes connected with your profession and changes that occur on a personal

19

or global level, which are entirely beyond your control, but can alter your life in a major way.

## *Change on a Personal and Social Level*

You could for example encounter one or more of the following changes in your private life:

falling in love

having a dream baby

buying a new house

getting your dream job

and other similar circumstances, all of which are happy or pleasant events and would obviously change you life completely for the better. These are welcome changes and you find you can adapt to each situation without any problem.

Traumatic personal changes in your life, however, over which you have no control, are quite a different story. How do you deal with a situation that upsets your life completely.

your partner wants a divorce

you have a stroke that leaves you half paralyzed

your loved one suddenly dies

you are crippled through an accident

you have an accident that leaves lifelong scars

and many other similar nightmares that influence your life in a major way. Where does the strength to deal with this come from?

## Change on an Economical Level

We can go through a few scenarios:

you begin the career of your dreams

you have the promotion you've been waiting for

you launch your own business

you win in the lottery

you inherit money

and you can imagine many more similar joyful scenarios.

Once again these are all pleasant exciting changes and you would have no difficulty to accept and to adapt to the new situation. But when the changes are bad news and without warning, for example:

you lose your job or source of income

you face bankruptcy

you lose all your savings in the money market

your life investments become worthless

and many other similar unhappy or disastrous situations.

What happens then? Suddenly you feel that your world has come to an abrupt standstill. You have no control. Thinking your world has collapsed and seeing no way out, you might even consider suicide for a moment. How do you handle that and to whom do you turn?

## *Change on a Global Level*

The last decades have brought radical changes to the world in which labor and capital operate and there is a greater recognition of the global, interdependent nature of economic forces than has ever existed before. The gap between rich and poor is becoming increasingly unacceptable as the people from the third world countries aspire towards a higher standard of living. New technology and satellite communications have transformed the labor market in a major way and the way that international business is conducted. Humanity as a whole is responding to a new vision of a global society which respects human rights and promotes the well being of people all over the world. The concentration is towards working on the transformation of humanity and to awakening to the right principles of sharing and distribution.

As the globe shrinks in size our own personal point of view needs to expand. We have to learn to be tolerant of cultures, languages, religions and beliefs that so far have been totally foreign to us. We are expected to empathize with people with whom we have up to the present, nothing in common with, and we are required to understand, tolerate or accept to share our way of life with them. Many people find this to be so difficult that they cannot and will not accept it, convinced that they can keep themselves intact in their own safe little cocoons by ignoring the world around them. This, however, is simply not possible. It is difficult to ignore what is happening around us. We need to understand that we, humanity, are all intertwined and our survival depends on each other. We need to understand that we, each one of us, is a part of a whole and each, in our own personal little way, has to contribute to the whole.

All changes personal, economical and global, will influence us personally and will leave a mark in our emotions and the only way for each one of us to deal with such times of extreme changes, is by concentrating and making an individual effort to look and face ourselves. We need to re-educate and prepare ourselves individually to learn to adapt, and this radical transformation in us, has to come from deep within ourselves. Our involvement and our actions must be conditioned by reflection and inner growth. The direction is in the consciousness of humanity towards the fusion of the individual with the whole, without losing at the same time the sense of individuality. The focus is, therefore, on none other than the 'Self.' The 'Self' is intangible, invisible but a very real part of you, is imprisoned in matter, your physical body, has to be freed and allowed out of matter and darkness and into the light. The Self can only manifest itself through your physical body. You can read more about the inner self in the chapter 'Know Thyself.'

Modern science has confirmed that all the information of life is contained in each cell of our body. When a person is born, this life carries complete detailed information in each cell according to a fixed plan. Growth, development and other functions are all preprogrammed. A human being is a system that has to develop, and from birth to death every human being has an inner urge to fulfill this program. Our body is nothing but a tool with one function, to help us reach a goal. Too many experiences, premonitions and sensations that transcend the material, rule over our lives and it is inner impulses that emerge which urge us forward to new thoughts, new ideas and new deeds. Resistance to the natural flow of things and evolution increases in proportion to the degree of our dogmatism. Lacking any discernible movement, this stagnation makes us inflexible and rigid.

Everything we see, hear and feel, everything we consider as good or bad on the outside, is the result of our own inner transformation. If we observe ourselves our speech, our attitude and the reaction of others we will soon realize that according to our own behavior, we are either increasing our problems or we are helping to solve them. If we watch this part of our lives carefully we will soon be aware of the many opportunities life offers us and the many that we miss. With persistence and avoidance of prejudices, bitterness and fixed ideas, even if we fail time and again to begin with, we will ultimately gain clarity of thought. Flexibility and clarity of thought, combined with intelligence and goodwill will produce constructive action. Constructive thoughts and constructive actions do not only make us personally happier but also all of those who are around us as well. Our family, friends, society and everyone we come in contact with. Remember the ripple effect.

*Some of us thrive on change and move on*
*looking forward and enjoying life,*
*others hold on for dear life to status quo*
*stay behind and suffer.*

# 5

# Approaches to Change

Rudolf Steiner comments in his book Inner Aspect of the Social Question, *'...how extraordinarily banal it is to say: 'We live in a time of transition.' All times are times of transition! The point is not to call this or that period a time of transition; the point is to see what is involved in a particular change or transition. That is the essential thing; to perceive what is changing!'*

The physicist, Fritjof Capra, in his book The Turning Point writes of the new holistic world view emerging in the field: *'In the twentieth century physics has gone through several conceptual revolutions that clearly reveal the limitations of the mechanistic world view and lead to an organic, ecological view of the world which shows great similarities to the views of the mystic of all ages and traditions. The universe is no longer seen as a machine, made up of a multitude of separate objects, but appears as a harmonious indivisible whole; a network of dynamic relationships that include the human observer and his or her consciousness in an essential way. The fact that modern physics, the manifestation of an extreme specialization of the rational mind, is now making contact with mysticism, the essence of religion and manifestation of an extreme specialization of the intuitive mind, shows very beautifully the unity and complementary nature of the rational and intuitive modes of consciousness; of the yang and the yin. Physicists, therefore, can provide the scientific background to the changes in attitudes and values that our society so urgently needs. In a culture dominated by science, it will be much easier to convince our social institutions that fundamental changes are necessary if we can give our arguments a scientific basis. That is what physicists can now provide. Modern physics can show the other sciences that scientific thinking does not necessarily have to be reductionism and mechanistic, that holistic and ecological views are also scientifically sound.'*

Nothing is different about us having to live with change. What has altered very dramatically in the past decades is that, changes are now imposed upon us so rapidly that we hardly have time to digest and adapt ourselves to one new idea, before we are confronted with the next one. We find ourselves having to re-adjust our thoughts and patterns of behavior over and over again. This can be very disconcerting and tiring, for those of us who are accustomed to dealing with change, or even for those characters that thrive on change. This, however, can be very traumatic for those of us who have been lulled into an easy comfortable existence.

As we grow up, we are always challenged to widen our horizon and adapt in many both minor and in major ways. Yet, as we reach adulthood, most of us settle down to a regular life style with less and less allowance for change. Intentionally or unintentionally, we settle down to a comfortable way of living, an existence with the minimum of challenge, and we remain quite comfortable with this slumbering routine, until some external hand strikes a blow and a new situation is forced upon us waking us up rudely from our sleep. We are then caught off guard and like it or not, we have to deal with the situation. Shaken out of our secure existence, we are angry, annoyed, frustrated and more often than not we lose our control.

Those of us who have a personality with an open mind, a positive attitude and flexibility of thought are better equipped and able to handle change better than others are. Those of us who thrive on change, and stagnation means mental deterioration, when finding ourselves in a rut, we take matters into our own hands and deliberately create changes in our lives, accepting the consequences.

Whatever phase of change is confronting you, there are only two choices. You either choose to be passive, stubbornly ignoring it, avoiding or blocking it. Or you can actively take matters into your own hands and be in control of your life.

*The two Approaches to Change*
*The Negative or the Positive Approach*

## *The Negative Approach—*

In any unhappy situation, in your private life or at work, for example, a marriage turned sour, an unhappy relationship, getting older, being unemployed or in an unsatisfactory job, a health problem, or anything that you feel dissatisfied with, you can be passive and take a negative approach. You can
-become addicted to drugs or alcohol to help you dull your senses. You can pretend your problem does not exist and you can carry on with your life as it is, for as long as possible.
-resign yourself to a monotonous existence, wallowing in self-pity, feeling victimized.

-Get angry, complain and blame others for your hurt shifting all responsibility away from your shoulders on to someone else.

-Become hyper active, running around keeping yourself busy with an overload of senseless activities, convincing yourself of their importance or necessity and avoid the problem until you end up with a heart attack or an accident.

Any excuse, any escape is good enough as long as you do not have to face the unpleasant reality and you do not have to take action.


## *The Positive Approach—*


You can, on the other hand, decide to act, to take the positive approach, take your life in your own hands, have trust in yourself and in life, and have confidence in your ability to begin all over again, no matter what it takes.

This active approach requires a lot of effort, perhaps some sacrifices and plain hard work. It is definitely a tougher road to take but it is the most rewarding. This road begins with you having to confront yourself and to work on changing yourself, your views, values and beliefs. To do this you have to be fully committed, physically, emotionally and mentally so that you can adapt to the new circumstances. Taking this approach has its many rewards. Taking this approach and acting upon it you activate powers within you that give you tremendous inner strength and you will discover and rediscover a new power within you which you never thought you had until you eventually emerge each time, a totally new person with many new valuable qualities.

We cannot change outside circumstances in our lives but we can control our own feelings, our attitudes, our actions and our circumstances. We can take control of a situation and accept the responsibility for our decisions.

What is important is to recognize the difference between the two types of changes. Some changes we can control deliberately, other changes are enforced upon us. The changes enforced upon us, we are unable to control and we have no other choice but to accept them and to shift our concentration to changing ourselves in order to deal creatively with our new life and the new set of circumstances. Knowing and understanding this difference makes it easier for us, to make our choice of actions.

*We are all guilty of inertia and procrastination*
*We all carry our past with us*
*in one way or another.*
*We are all slaves of our habits*
*and our actions are the result*
*of how we have been conditioned.*
*That's the bad news.*

*The good news is*
*It is within our power to change ourselves!*

# 6

# Seven Obstacles to Change

Here are seven major reasons why people resist change. See if you can recognize yourself anywhere.

*Inertia, Procrastination, Hanging on the Past, Habit, Fear, Lack of Self Esteem and Lack of Faith.*

## Inertia —

*Let's face it – we are all by nature lazy.*

Inertia comes in different forms, we can be physically lazy, and we can also be mentally or emotionally lazy. Resistance to change is often nothing more than just being too lazy to make the effort it takes to deal with change. It requires effort to extend yourself in order to handle change. It requires you to move out of your being comfortable, the space referred to as your 'comfort zone,' and to take action. First it takes emotional energy to accept and to deal with the process. Then you have to exert mental energy to work out an action plan and then physical energy to actively carry out the plan. In most cases though, people look for an easy way out and a way of least resistance, a way that requires the minimum of effort or preferably no effort at all.

Laziness exists in each and every one of us without exception in varied degrees. No matter how energetic and ambitious we may be, some laziness will be lurking somewhere in us, if we allow it. Laziness, I think, is the basic adversity that is born in all of us and one of the major challenges that we have to overcome during our lifetime. Not only the physical laziness. We often procrastinate because we are too lazy to face unpleasant reality becoming slaves to our bad habits and ingrained thoughts.

Inertia has many faces and has nothing to do with how many hours you work on your job or how active you are with your hobbies. You can be seemingly busy doing many unimportant tasks that do not tax your energy, in order to avoid doing other more urgent but unpleasant tasks that need your attention. Non-communication, fear, stubbornness, being inflexible and unable to adapt, avoiding commitment and responsibility are all forms of laziness, and the lazier we are the lazier we become.

Those who are more open to growth are more aware of their laziness and do whatever they can to check it and to keep it under control. This is achieved by being aware, making a continuous daily effort and being persistently in control of yourself and your life. The more you manage to overcome some of your laziness, the more you become aware of yourself being lazy. So in time, the less lazy you get, the more aware you are of yourself and the more effort you will exert. Once you realize and accept this and make an effort to fight it, you will discover a whole new rich existence.

One good way to check on yourself and your state of inertia is by observing yourself for one day and taking note of how often you choose to take the easier way of doing things. The way that requires the least effort from you. The next day you can check yourself by focusing on one small task and you choose a way which would require you to exert a little extra effort. For example, you make a point of being very friendly and take time to chat over a few pleasantries, with a person whom you do not particularly think is important for you and whom you hardly ever bother to talk to normally. Or you can make an extra effort, coming out of yourself, to be very friendly and understanding towards someone in your family circle, whom you usually dislike intensely, afraid of, jealous of, or someone whom you are angry with. In this way, you would be involved with your emotions actively. Observe yourself and your feeling as you do this emotional exercise.

On the physical level, you can for example, walk up the stairs instead of using the elevator. Or walk to the restaurant to lunch instead of using the car. Going for a walk and have a sandwich instead of sitting in a restaurant. On a mental level you could read a book instead of watching TV on Sunday. Or you could go to a museum or a cultural evening, concert or opera, instead of going for a drink. These are just a few examples of how you can become aware of your laziness and operating through habit. The idea is to do something that demands more effort than what you are habitually willing to give.

## Procrastination—

*'I'll do it tomorrow'*

We all procrastinate at one time or another.

All of us are guilty of procrastination and it happens in many shapes and forms, in any course of our life. Both minor and major decisions are put off, because we don't feel comfortable with them. We are not sure what to do, or we dislike the issue at hand, so we procrastinate, secretly hoping by putting it off that the problem will either solve itself or will get forgotten or better still, will just disappear.

When you have a problem you find particularly unpleasant to solve, for whatever reason you procrastinate. Every day you convince yourself that you have other priorities that you should be dealing with first, leaving you no free time. Your problem could be an unpleasant one and you don't want to face it, or you are not sure how to deal with it exactly; or it is just too difficult a problem for you to handle, so you avoid it. You have it on your mind and you suffer from a constant nagging feeling of guilt but you continue anyway to put it aside, promising yourself that you will deal with it tomorrow. And every tomorrow you think of another excuse why you cannot. It is true in some cases, time can work miracles and sometimes might even bring a solution. This depends on the problem at hand. Mostly, however, the longer you put off a problem, the worse it becomes, the more complicated it will be to solve it and the more you will hurt and suffer.

As a procrastinator you are constantly putting off things that you should be attending to, making extensive lists of things you should do and then never having the time to get around to doing any of them. Consider the fact that you might be continuing a pattern of your inner child reacting to coercive directions of your parents. Many of us were exposed to a constant attack of 'don't do this!' or 'must you do that now!' and 'why don't you listen to me!' etc. in our childhood. Although the parents mean well the child reacts with active resistance. An endless cycle begins with the constant unhappy nagging and directing and the child's escape to find refuge in day dreaming and doodling. Such behavior continues automatically in adulthood and resisting, stalling and finding excuses of why we can't attend to things that we should be attending to are always there. This is the cause of much unnecessary unhappiness and self-defeating behavior.

There is a way to train yourself to get over this putting-off thing till later habit. To free yourself of this nagging feeling, which has become a negative energy and therefore a heavy burden to carry, holding you back, you can decide right now to do something about it. Not tomorrow, not later, but right here and now. You can begin immediately to take control by picking one small task that you have been putting off, any small task, and make a point of attending to it today, right now. It is important to choose a smaller task to begin with, as it is easier to get it done with. Perhaps its a phone call you've been putting off for a while, which you should take care of and your conscious is nagging you constantly, but some odd reason you're not doing it. Take a deep breath pick up the phone and do it now. Perhaps you have a closet, a filing cabinet or a garage that you should be clearing out. Perhaps it is a letter you should be writing, or even a movie you have intended to see but never found the time. Perhaps it is that massage that you need for your backache but you keep telling yourself you can't afford it, just pick one task from your 'should do' list and do it now. This gives you self-satisfaction, a feeling which once you have tasted, you would like to repeat again and again.

Being satisfied with oneself for having accomplished something is a very pleasant feeling. Make a note of another task that you want to accomplish tomorrow. The next day you pick up this other small task, that you have been meaning to take care of for a long time, and before the day is over, you have it done. Again you will be encouraged by enjoying this feeling of accomplishment. Reward yourself with a little something that makes you happy. Rewarding yourself is an important gesture because it is usually your lower consciousness that refuses to cooperate. Every one likes to have a pat on the back for doing a good job. Repeat this every day, one small task at a time. Then pick up a larger task, a more complicated problem that might need more effort and more time. Your reward to yourself should be in accordance with your task. The bigger the effort you make, the bigger your reward should be to yourself.

It is the qualities of a positive attitude, courage and trust, enthusiasm and will power that help us to overcome procrastination. The more we maximize these feelings in ourselves the better we will be able to deal with our problems.

## Hanging on to the Past—

*We all carry our past around with us,*
*where we differ, however, is how and*
*which part of our past we carry with us.*

Hanging on to the past, is a favorite pastime for many of us who like to blame our origin, our parents, or others for all our misfortunes in life. We continue all our lives blaming everyone else and circumstances for everything that goes wrong for us. We refuse to take responsibility for our actions or for that matter for our non-actions.

We carry an invisible huge bag with us, full of resentment, anger, self-pity, hate, envy, jealousy, criticism and we willingly keep adding to the burden along our journey in life making our load heavier and heavier as we go along, making us feel more and more miserable. We are in a continuous state of hopelessness and we make everyone with whom we come into contact just as miserable as ourselves. We live buried in the past and make little effort to relate to the present. This attitude and behavior is usually a one-way ticket to disaster, illness, loss of job, loss of friends or family.

The important point to remember is that you are who you are today because of your origin and your own life experiences. Your experiences in life, whether positive or negative, can always be a source of benefit to you. If you have a sincere desire to move in a more positive direction, you must change your attitude regarding your past unhappiness. Storing these in your memory causes you to back away from making a sincere effort to move forward or to succeed. Playing the role of victim of the past is self-indulgent, self-destructive and non-productive. It is also one way of escaping living in the present. How can you live and enjoy or experience the present moment if you are always thinking of and reliving the past?

You cannot change your past, but you can change your attitude toward your past. You can read more on this in the chapter 'Free Yourself of Your Chains.' You alone determine your mental attitude. You alone are responsible for your feelings about the past. Develop awareness so that you can leave all the unpleasant and hurtful experiences in your life behind you and take with you only the pleasant and happy memories that make you feel good. Instead of weighing yourself down with sad unhappy hurtful memories, have your bag full of light happy joyful memories that will act in the future, as a well of warmth and strength for you. In times of trouble of loneliness which we all experience, you can sit back and draw on these memories for comfort, whenever you are in trouble, feel low or alone. Many people make the mistake of giving too much power to the past and this can cause a lot of stress in your life. It is true, what you did yesterday will have an influence on what you do today. However, this also means that what you do today, will have an influence on what happens to you tomorrow.

Changing your attitude towards the past can free you from much anger, resentments and bitterness. Accept your past for whatever it was and understand it, whether you contributed to it or not, good or bad, it was what it was and it is now over and gone. It cannot be repeated and you cannot change it. If it was an unhappy experience, learn from it whatever lessons you can, or accept it as an experience which will perhaps make sense much later on in your life. I, personally, am of the belief that there are no coincidences in life and everything that happens, has a meaning. This might not always be apparent immediately, but some time or the other I am able to think back and I understand. This belief, for me, helps me to accept the negative experiences in my life without burdening myself with unpleasant feelings. Contemplate on your past and see for yourself if this is not the case for you as well.

More likely you have many happy joyful memories that you have forgotten about while you were busy concentrating on the sad and hurtful memories. Shift your focus consciously and draw on your store of happy memories gradually and keep your focus there for as long as you can. This will eventually overpower the sad and less joyful experiences and you will gradually begin to heal. Should you, however, have a past that you have to date been unable to come to terms with, then perhaps this is the time to seek professional help to assist you and to show you how you can digest these unpleasant feelings and throw the cobwebs out of your system. There are many natural alternative modern healing methods known today that can help you to cleanse your system out, physically, emotionally and mentally.

## Habit—

*We are all creatures of habit.*
*But it is within our power to control our habits.*

We humans are creatures of habit and we are all slaves to our habits far more than we realize. We are very quick to acquire habits, in particular bad habits, and we stick with them throughout our lives, unless change forces us to forsake them and acquire new ones. More often than not even more bad habits. Many of us leave it up to chance and circumstances and never learn to take matters into our own hands to change our bad habits into good habits. Many of us are unaware that it is within our power to change our habits.

Often, even if we know we are doing a certain thing out of habit and even if we know it is not good for us, we keep on doing it, feeling powerless to change it. Often we say 'well, this is

45

the way I am.' We can make a habit of living in the past or of being fearful. We can make a habit of constantly worrying about something or the other, without reason. We can be in the habit of being always inconsiderate, angry and resentful. It is only when a force outside of ourselves takes over in some way to exert influence over us, that we are obliged to wake up out of these habits and we are left with no choice but to react. This can appear in the form of a serious illness, an accident, a divorce, or a loss of a job, more often than not self inflicted. With self-awareness, we can learn that we are able to make our own choices and decisions and we can, if we really want to, also get rid of most of our bad habits and acquire some good habits instead.

Habit is the opposite of awareness. When you are doing anything out of habit, what it actually means is that you are on automatic pilot with the real you pushed away, dormant and inactive. In other words, your body, the machine, is operating on its own. The real you is left out and is uninvolved. You can literally live your whole life in this manner. Imagine how much of life you would be missing out on, if this were true for you. Let me tell you this funny story I heard in a workshop I attended many years ago in New

York, as a good example for old habits that do not make any sense.

Mary and Jack were newly wed and Mary was cooking her first Sunday dinner, pot roast. She cut the roast in half before she put it in a tray then into the oven. Jack was watching and he asked why she cut the roast before she put it in the oven. Mary said, *'Oh, I don't really know, but my Mom always does that, so I do it too!'* Next day while Mary was having a chat on the phone with her Mom, she asked, *'Mom, by the way, why do you always cut the roast in half before you cook it?'* and her mother replied, *'I don't know Mary but I do it because I saw Granny always doing it, so I do it too.'* Mom called Granny. *'Mother, why do you cut the roast before you put it into the oven?'* and Granny said, *'Well, it's just a habit dear, you see, in the old days, the family was so large, I had to cut the huge piece of roast in half, otherwise it wouldn't fit into the small over!'*

Talk about habit! You see something, you do not question, you do not think, you copy and you do the same. With no awareness of what or why you are doing it. Because Mary was accustomed to her mother cutting the roast, she copied and she continued the habit. Imagine how many habits we might have that we carry down through generations, that are outdated and make no sense at all. You might have a thought pattern, an attitude or a feeling that is based on old-fashioned beliefs of your parents. These might have served a purpose at the time. You continue this habit today into your adult life and even pass on to your own children without questioning its origin or validity. This could be hampering your growth process or even limiting your existence and experience of life, but because it is so ingrained in you, it is a part of you that you do not even think of questioning. Living with awareness means you observe and question your every thought and action. This requires great mental effort, and usually the greater the effort the greater the reward.

## *Fear—*

*We all experience fear at one time or another*
*even the most courageous of us.*
*Some of us, however, live in a constant state of fear.*

Fear is one major reason for not accepting change. Fear of the unknown, fear of being ridiculed. Fear of losing a job or losing a loved one. Fear of getting old or of dying. Fear of poverty, being rejected or being alone. Fear of not being loved but most of all fear of the new and fear of all that is foreign and unfamiliar. Fear leads to resentment and anger, anger leads to hate and hate leads to suffering. Fear is actually a product of ignorance.

Fear is like a disease, it is a negative emotion, the same as jealousy, envy or hate. If we allow fear to take over our emotions, it could destroy us including everyone we deal with because, fear is an emotion and emotions are contagious. Fear can become a monster eating us up inside and can paralyze the senses and the intellect. When we are afraid we are incapable of rational thinking, of having an opinion or of making a rational decision, we are also incapable of taking any kind of intelligent action. Fear, which generates anger and the need to control, is a major obstacle to growth that we need to confront and put aside.

We have to be careful not to make a habit of being fearful. Insecurity and lack of confidence can be a source of constant fear. For example, if I am a professional, I am in constant fear of saying the wrong thing or making the wrong decisions. Perhaps I am afraid a meeting will go wrong, or that I lose a client. Even worse I might be in constant fear of losing my job. If I am entertaining I might be afraid of burning the dinner. If I am invited, I might be afraid of not being appropriately dressed. If I am a student I might be afraid that no one will like me. I am afraid that I will fail my exam. I am afraid my husband will leave me, or I am afraid my wife will cheat on me, and the list can go on and on. But having read this far, notice that this fear has to do mostly with 'me' and 'myself' and 'my' fear of this or that. If, however, I were to shift my focus to concentrate on the other party instead, I would forget myself as being the center of attention. I would automatically forget my fears and be relaxed. I would be interested and involved instead in the person, group, environment, work, or conversation and I would probably enjoy myself so much that there would be no room for my fear in my emotions. For example, instead of worrying what to say or how I say it, I would focus on listening to what others have to say and reply when I have something to say. Instead of worrying how I look I would compliment others on their looks. If I have a job to deliver, I would concentrate on doing it well. Instead of feeling insecure I would consecrate on making others feel comfortable. Instead of criticizing I would try to understand, have tolerance and compassion.

Love is the opposite emotion of fear. The more we are able to fill our heart and life with love, the less room there would be for fear. All of us are capable of much more love than we allow ourselves to feel. Most of us tend to confine love to a partner or a few family members or a pet. What we need to do is to fill our hearts with love for the self and then to extend this out to the world around us and every one in it. Promoting the feeling of compassion in ourselves is a beginning to fill our heart and our life with love. Love promotes courage, curiosity, enthusiasm and understanding. Knowledge and understanding eliminate ignorance and fear. Fear is like a beast always lurking around you and in you ready to pounce on you. We have all experienced our inner monsters. You have a choice, you can live forever trembling in fright every time this inner monster shows up, hiding and cowering paralyzed or you can put on your fighting armor and finally decide to turn around and to face this inner monster, to fight it and overpower it till it is dead and gone out of your life. If your monsters are too big for you to deal with, don't be afraid or too proud to seek help. It is possible to live a life free of fear.

The qualities you need to practice here to replace your fear are open mindedness, tolerance, understanding, compassion, faith and love.

## Lack of Self Esteem —

*We all, even the most confident of us,*
*have some moments of low self-esteem.*

A combination of self-confidence and self-esteem empowers a person to keep moving forward and upward. An individual can experience a devastating loss, conquer it and emerge from it more triumphant than before with self-confidence and self esteem. If you feel, however, insecure and have low self esteem, you would be incapable to handle changes in your life well, to take the right decisions because you are unsure and you are afraid to take any risk. Naturally, change would be for you totally undesirable.

Low self-esteem is a result of not accepting yourself as you are and not recognizing your strengths nor your weaknesses. You can neither maximize on your strengths nor guard your weaknesses and as a result you cannot take control of your life. Lack of self-confidence robs you of your independence, making you lean on others to guide you through life. Having low self-esteem could be due to the way you have been programmed in your youth. It could be the result of one or more unhappy experiences in your life which you have not been able to digest. There could be a multitude of reasons and again it is entirely within your power to change that. It is in your hands to work on yourself to gain self-confidence. Remember that insecurity is not a permanent condition and you have the power to choose, rather than berating yourself dwelling on your inadequacies and weaknesses maximize your strengths instead. Accept new challenges in your life and practice with small projects, which you are sure to be able to overcome. To develop your self-esteem connect with people who affirm your gifts and talents and avoid those who criticize you or belittle you. Remember it is people with low self- esteem who usually criticize others in order to feel better about themselves. Practice self-forgiveness when you make mistakes, do not be too harsh on yourself and do not allow failure to destroy your self-esteem. Every successful person has gone through many failures. Even the most confident person can feel insecure now and again.

Self-confident people are normally relaxed and feel comfortable with themselves. Therefore, they feel comfortable with others everywhere. They are usually friendly, considerate, understanding. Arrogance is very often mistaken for self-confidence. In reality though, this is far from true. It is insecurity that makes a person behave with arrogance. Self-confident people have no need to be arrogant nor to criticize or judge others. On the contrary, they have respect both for themselves and for everyone around them as well. A person who acts with arrogance, disrespect and inconsideration towards others is displaying insecurity, lack of self-confidence and low self-esteem. Keep this in mind and the next time you meet with an arrogant or inconsiderate person you can smile with understanding and compassion because you know the arrogance is nothing but a camouflage for personal insecurities. The more you control and minimize negativity in you the more self-esteem you will gain and the more self confident you will be.

## Lack of Faith—

*All of us have questioned our beliefs at some stage in our lives, perhaps even lost our faith altogether during the process of growing up.*

In all you do and whatever religious belief you have, an important ingredient is missing in your life if you have no faith. Believing and having faith in yourself and in a Higher Power gives you inner strength.

Perhaps you were raised in a family where religion played a big role. Perhaps you were disillusioned as you grew older and rebelled the only way you knew how, by going to the other extreme and renouncing faith in God altogether. Or due to peer pressure you joined the group of atheists, who denied spirituality and God. Perhaps deep down in yourself you do believe in something but you are not sure what exactly to believe in. Perhaps due to past conditioning you think that whatever you have faith in, must be represented in an image form. Perhaps you have no one whom you can trust to talk to about your most private thoughts and doubts.

When speaking to people who are successful in life, in any field, you inevitably find that they project an inner strength and wisdom and all without exception, believe in their own spirituality. They follow a set of personal values and moral ethics from which they do not waver. They all, without exception, are aware and respect a Higher Power above them and recognize an inner power within them from which they gather their strength.

Faith has nothing to do with religion nor does faith have any barriers of gender, color, race or culture. Faith cannot be taught nor can it forced on you. Faith is an inner feeling, a very personal, individual experience. It is a spiritual experience. Being religious and being spiritual are two separate things. Everyone and everything that is in motion, moving forward, straining for the better and the higher is spiritual. We all have had at least once, if not more, an experience of ecstasy when something has gone exactly our way, of being totally alive and aware and we feel with all of our being, in tune with all around us and at one with the universe. We feel the miracle of being alive, the miracle of the birth of a perfect baby, the wonder and perfection of the universe, we appreciate the perfect beauty of a flower, we are in a moment of bliss, we fall in love and so on. We sense, we feel and we know of the existence of a Higher Force, a Higher Intelligence that is much stronger and much mightier than we are. We are at one with our self and this self experience is a divine reality in every one of us to discover individually without the help of dogma or creed, imposed on us by an organized religion, group, or Guru. It is fine to seek knowledge, to listen and learn but remain always true to your own self and listen to your own inner voice.

When we are really alive we feel love and joy in our heart and when we feel love we have faith. Faith and trust in life and in ourselves. Faith cannot be analyzed with the intellect nor can it be touched or seen, it can only be felt within. It is a psychic experience. We all know the expression 'faith can move mountains' and most of us have been witness to 'faith working miracles.' Faith works like an anchor giving you a strong hold, and inner peace, It is a great source of strength. Have faith and trust in yourself.

*You can change at any moment in your life.*
*Any moment is the right time.*
*It is entirely up to you.*

# 7

# Three Elements for Change

The three major qualities that are needed so that you can achieve change in yourself and your life are the three Ds. A deep and genuine DESIRE, an unshakable DISCIPLINE and a DETERMINATION to persist until you have achieved your goal.

## *Desire—*

*As Napolean Hills said, '"Dreams come true when desire transforms them into concrete action. Ask life for great gifts and you encourage life to deliver them to you."* Many decisions to change a habit fail and many goals are never achieved simply because the decision is made on a conscious level with intellect alone. You decide intellectually to do something and then you begin to find thousand excuses why you cannot follow through and then you wonder why you don't get to where you want to go. The intention was there but what was missing here is the genuine inner passionate desire. The passionate desire comes from your emotional level that was in this case not committed to support your intentions. You may be able to put up pretence for a few days but because emotions are stronger than intellectual intentions, sooner or later, your inner feelings get the better of you and you give up.

This passionate desire deep within combined with total commitment must be there. Thinking and speaking, or wishing and hoping, about your waiting to change is not enough. I am sure you can remember some incident in your life when you felt a great longing to achieve something and you actually did. Very often when you feel a real genuine desire for something, you will observe, that you tend to keep it a secret for yourself and not talk about it. You go ahead and do whatever needs to be done, without discussing it with anyone. Your whole attention is focused on your goal. You focus with all your might and not only think it but you literally breathe it, feel it, touch it, imagine it, see it, as if you had it already. You cannot imagine yourself without it. It is when you feel this exactly, that you know your desire is there and you are fully committed with every fiber of your body. Every one of us has felt this some time or another. You know you want something and you know that you are going to get it without fail.

When you have a deeply ingrained desire for something, you usually instinctively keep your attention on your goal throughout the day and night, even while you are carrying on with your daily chores, until you get the result you desire. It is possible, if you wish, to consciously help program your emotions with affirmations and pictures. You can help yourself to introduce this desire to achieve a certain goal, through several methods. You can write down your goal to the last very minute detail and look at some pictures, to inspire you, of things similar to your goal every night before you go to sleep. Along with that you can also repeat daily suitable affirmations. When writing your affirmations remember to make sure that the sentences are precise and clear in the present and positive tense. For example, you could say:

My life is in perfect order

Everything good is coming to me now

I love my life

I am happy and content

I am successful in everything I do

I am prosperous

I am healthy

I am a warm and loving person

I am free of anger and resentments

I attract loving people to me

I am free of the desire to smoke

I am slim and free of all excess fat

Be sure to keep your affirmations positive. For example do not say:

I do not smoke or I am not fat etc.

Affirmations should also always be practical and they should have good intentions. They should also have to do only with you. Do not even think about an affirmation involving someone else to do something for you. You cannot affirm for example, I want Mary or Max to love me or marry me, and I want my employer to give me a bonus etc. It will not work! Affirmations will not work if you are tense or angry and you want to force an issue. The purpose of affirmation is to talk yourself into believing that you are what you want to be, or you have what you want to have.

You have to be practical and intelligent about this though and not affirm something that is impossible. I mean, it would be kind of silly, if I have brown eyes, to say I now have blue eyes! It would be more logical and practical for me to go out and to buy blue contact lenses! Try it out with little things that you know are possible for you to achieve, but you fail the energy, the courage or the means to carry it through. Affirm one sentence, write it down on a small piece of paper and stick it on the mirror in your bathroom and next to your bed or in your car to remind you. Begin with a simple, I love life. I am happy and content. Repeat this to yourself as many times as possible throughout the day and watch yourself after three or four weeks. You will probably surprise yourself to see a happy and content person who loves life!

Using your imagination and visualizing your wish is important to go with your affirmation. As you are saying your affirmation to achieve a goal, visualize yourself in that scene, in your mind's eye see yourself in that way. You see yourself happy, full of joy for being alive, you see yourself content. Whether your eyes are closed or open that is how you imagine yourself. If you visualize this long enough and often enough, and accompany it with your thoughts and affirmations, very soon the same picture will manifest in the physical form and you will become that person. Whatever it is that you want to visualize or affirm must be for the good of all concerned, i.e. no one must get hurt or come to any harm in any way by that which you affirm or visualize for yourself.

I would like to explain the contradiction between desire as we understand it as necessary in order to reach a goal and in Buddhism where we are told, that we can only be happy if we are free of desire. Let's understand what the word desire means. To desire is to wish, to fancy, to want, to long for, to yearn, to hunger for, to be greedy, to grasp and to crave. But desire also means to aspire, to seek, to aim and to strive. Note the negative connotation in the first part that has to do more with taking in and to withhold for oneself and the obvious positive implication in the latter part. To aspire, to seek, to aim and to strive can be said to be a spiritual process because it has to do with moving forward, reaching out and growing. The natural process of evolution of the human being takes place naturally over millions or thousands of years, but with aspiration and strive one can expedite the process of transformation moving on towards higher consciousness.

There is a difference, therefore, in what it is that I desire or aspire for. The difference is my motive, the reason I desire how I go about reaching my goal and what I plan to do once I have achieved the result. I personally, make sure that whatever it is that I aspire for, is not only beneficial for me but for all others concerned as well. In other words I am aware of what it is that I desire, because I know that, when I go against the law of nature, or against the flow of my life stream, my own desire can boomerang on me and hurt me. I do not desire to gain for myself at the expense of others.

## *Discipline —*

Once your desire is established and your goal is clear to you, what you need next is to have the discipline to carry your plan through to completion. This means you have to take charge of yourself and discipline yourself to make a plan of action, and to carry out this plan step by step, no matter what it requires. Desiring something alone, without actually taking action on the physical level, does not bring you any result. You need to be firm with yourself and not allow yourself to be sidetracked.

Discipline means reflecting and informing yourself first on what you require to do exactly so that you can achieve your goal. Then you lay out a detailed daily plan for yourself to do whatever has to be done and you make sure that you adhere to this plan without exception. Try not to talk too much about your plans or else you run the risk of someone talking you out of it and your energy will not be focused. Surround yourself instead with people who will support you and encourage you to achieve your goal and to avoid so called friends who hinder you by discouraging you. Sometimes family members and in particular close friends are more of a hindrance than help because they may criticize you and urge you to give up. They might mean well with their advice but in fact they are instilling doubt in your mind. Be aware of the difference between those who genuinely help you with constructive criticism, inspiring and motivating you to go on, and those who block you with destructive criticism.

Asking for advice is fine to get another point of view, but limit the number down to two or three people. Choose someone whom you know cares about you, or even a stranger, and a therapist perhaps. Reflect on all the advice that you get and only then you make up your own mind. Remember it is your life and you have to live it. You are the one who is ultimately responsible for your actions because it is you who will have to deal with consequences.

One thing important to keep in mind as far as discipline is concerned. Even discipline has to be disciplined. Try to stay on a middle course and not to carry your discipline to extremes. Any idea or action that is taken to an extreme will ultimately be negative and lead to a closed mind. By all means be committed and concentrate your energy on your goal but do not be a fanatic about it. Be firm with your discipline but rational and reasonable in what you demand of yourself. Get a sense for the flow of things, use your common sense and determine just how disciplined you need to be. When you meet with too many obstacles for instance, then take it as a sign that you could be on the wrong track, recognize this to be a sign to take a step back and to reevaluate your actions and outside forces. Think of the saying, for everything to be perfect, you have to be at the right place, at the right time and doing the right thing. If you do not sense this harmony then let go and stand back and wait for a while in spite of the deep desire you might be feeling. Stop to reconsider perhaps that which you desire so much is not the right thing for you after all. Again it is important to be reasonable about the amount of hindrances and obstacles that you might encounter. Don't give up too soon— this is where it is wise to practice plain common sense and sensitivity.

There is a Chinese parable, which advises to be flexible like a tree, and to bend according to the way the wind is blowing. If the tree stands too stiff and inflexible, it will snap when the wind blows too strong. Even high rise buildings are built so that they can sway with the wind. Sometimes you might have to adapt to whatever pressures occur along the way, perhaps even forcing you to sidetrack a little from your path. As long as you keep your goal in sight and you keep alert when the right opportunity shows itself, you can go back to your track heading towards your original goal. Sometimes we need to be alert because things might just work out differently and fate gives us something else than what we desire which is much better and suitable for us.

## *Determination —*

The third element of importance is the determination to go through to your goal, no matter what it takes. This means concentration, persistence; repetition and going on in spite of many setbacks that are bound to occur on your way. This needs tremendous will power and patience. Whether your progress is slow, fast or non-existent, and you are bound to experience all three stages again and again, you have to be determined to persist and to go on with your plan of action until all obstacles are overcome and you have achieved your goal.

Usually the way to a goal once you have made your decision, is easy to begin with, then you encounter some obstacles that you quickly get over and you go on. Then things might flow easy again for a while and you see yourself nearing your goal and you get tempted to relax your discipline a little. But then the goal seems to get further away, and you get tired, exhausted or fed up and now you are tempted to give up. There is usually one last and toughest hurdle of all just before the goal is reached requiring you to exert an extra amount of energy and effort. Very often this is exactly where most people give up and only the few who practice discipline and great determination make it to the end.

Normally in whatever task you have at hand, whether it is building a machine, walking up a mountain, playing baseball or tennis, learning a language, learning a new task or to ski, almost everyone goes through the same experience. At the point when you think you cannot possibly make it any more and you begin to doubt your own ability to succeed, it is crucial at this very moment, that you gather all your strength to keep on and not to give up. When you make this effort to persist and to keep on going, you surprise yourself by producing an extra load of energy that gives you the ability to get over this last obstacle taking you through to your goal. The point when you persist, you surpass your own level of energy automatically activating a reservoir of energy within you. It works the same way as the reserve tank of fuel in a car. In chapter 9 you can read more about this.

In summary your desire must be coupled with disciplined action and both desire and action need your determination and persistence to carry you through to the goal and all three qualities must generate from within you. To some people this comes naturally, others have to learn this and work hard at it. The same approach is taught worldwide to business executives and managers.

I would like to share with you a personal story, which I find a perfect example to demonstrate Desire, Discipline and Determination. This story is about my daughter, Zaza (short for Isabelle), who at the age of twenty five had the desire of pursuing a secret dream that she had carried with her since she was a child. Apparently she never ever shared this dream with another soul. Not even with her identical twin sister Gabrielle. She kept it her secret until one day I got a phone call from her. She was living and working in Zurich at the time and I had just come back from New York to Switzerland.

'Mami', she sounded very excited. 'I've had enough. I can't stand it any more. I am giving up my job!' She continued and I listened. 'I hate this rat race. There are more important things in life than money and business, I'm bailing out.' She had a great job, with a great income, she was working on Bahnhofstrasse, the most exclusive area in Zurich, she was manager of her own personnel recruitment department, in short, she was at the height of her career at twenty five and going strong. The world was her oyster.

Zaza had been in Australia where for a few years, she had her own fashion boutique and although she was successful she gave it up. She was married a couple of years and she got divorced. So I was not exactly surprised when I heard this latest news, but I was very curious to know what she was going to be up to next. 'I want to study music,' she declared, 'I want to live my life with music!' 'That sounds great.' I said, 'do you have any plans?' 'Well, I've bought a piano and I'm going to start taking lessons again.' And, 'I want to sing. I want to learn to sing!' I plan to register in a music school.' She said. 'Wonderful Zaza, if that is what you want to do, do it.' I encouraged. However, No school in the area would accept her. 'Impossible, with no musical background, no one learns to sing at the age of twenty-five! You're twenty years too late!' They said. Her few years of playing the piano were not enough she was told. She was angry and felt challenged. The energy of anger is an excellent motivator! She found herself a private teacher and within a week she started her lessons. Every single day without fail Zaza practiced exercised and worked part time to pay for her expensive singing lessons. She practiced many long hours every single day. She sang, she improved her piano playing and over the years she learned music theory, she took courses in voice therapy, in breathing, in self-growth and Alexander technique. To exercise discipline and to gain control over her physical body and lethargy, she delivered newspapers every day at 4 am for one year. To exercise her will power she walked on hot coals once a month for one year. She also fasted regularly. Every single long day she had a full program and she sang her way through it all. I did not see much of her during this period; she never had the spare time. But every now and again she'd leave a song on my answering machine so I could follow her progress. She never had much money, she was not moving around in exclusive surroundings, she was not dressed in designer clothes any more, but she was happy. It was tough, it was frustrating and it was exhausting but she was determined. She started with classical opera and in time developed the most beautiful voice, surprising and delighting both herself and the family.

Now five years later, Zaza's life is full of music and song every single day. She fell in love with her life partner of three years who is a classical guitar teacher and composes his own music. From classical opera, to Latin music, to Jazz, to Brazilian songs! Zaza can sing it all with a strong professional beautiful voice. A voice that needs no loudspeakers, it is pure and powerful.

With desire, discipline and determination Zaza has now achieved what she had apparently dreamt of every night since she was a child. Today her world is filled with music, exactly as she had imagined and wanted it to be. While both she and her partner earn their living with music, she continues to practice, exercise and she takes lessons. The newest is that she is working on research to develop a new music therapy concept and a CD, but she's mum about that for now.

I have great admiration and am very happy for my daughter who did it all on her own. The road was long and tedious, full of many obstacles and hard work but she did it. She had a vision, she made a decision, she acted on it and against all the odds, she carried it firmly through to the goal. In the process, she went through several major inner transformations. A perfect example of desire, discipline and determination, plus a huge dose of faith in herself. The 'faith in herself' is the most important. There is a difference between dreaming or desiring and visualizing. Many dreams remain in the dream world and do not manifest simply because no action is taken and not enough effort is made on the physical level. Zaza's dream remained a dream until she decided to make it materialize on the physical level. There are several important messages in this story.

First, there was desire and a clear vision.

Second, a decision was made to act 'now', not tomorrow, not next month, but right now. Immediately. In spite of all the odds.

(Obviously there was a lot of thought and reflection until the moment the action was taken. Obviously the element of courage is necessary to make the move.)

Third, it is never too late to do what your heart truly desires.

The fourth is to share a plan with a supportive person or group where one can fall back on for encouragement. Every one of us needs that, no matter how old, experienced or how strong we are. No man is an island unto himself.

The fifth is 'to let go' of the old and to leave it behind without any regrets or resentments. Leave behind whatever could hold you back.

The sixth is about 'going with the flow.' Once the right decision and the right effort are made, the right situations, the right people and the means will materialize as required.

The seventh is faith – to have full faith in oneself and in the future and be prepared to take the consequences, come what may. Most of all be prepared to accept the consequences.

*(After all there was a chance that Zaza had no singing voice at all and she would have had to be strong enough to accept that! But at the least she could say, I tried.)*

Zaza followed her own inner most desire and vision, she let go of her past life and she was 'going with the flow' of her own life stream. She had faith in herself, she was willing to put in the effort and there was no room for fear or doubt. How could she go wrong?

A dream, passion, intensity and commitment, joy and sweat, that's what it takes. Our worst enemy is our own fear and our self-imposed prison.

I wonder how many have a secret dream and never find the courage and the strength to make it manifest. Either because they are discouraged or ridiculed by others or because they simply are afraid to break out of their own self imposed limitations.

Perhaps your secret desire, as far-fetched as it may seem, is probably that which you should be doing right now.

*NB. To up date this story seven years later, in case you are interested, Zaza is still singing and is now married to Reto, her classical guitar teacher, they have completed four CDs in the meantime and they both live and work and enjoy life together. She still practices diligently and sings Opera and her voice continues to improve!*

*Everything you need is within you.*

# 8

# Your in-born Assets

You do not have to search for anything outside of yourself. In a poem by Jalaludin Rumi, a famous Sufi Sage, he says: *'New organs of perception come into being as a result of necessity. Therefore, O man, increase your necessity, so that you may increase your perception.'* Everything that you need already exists within you. If you take the time and concentrate on yourself you will be able to discover the treasures that are present in you, given to you at birth, to be discovered by you. Some of these treasures that you carry around with you are your mind, your feelings and your faith in yourself.

## *Your Mind, Your Feelings and Your Faith*

### *Your Mind —*

Sariputta, one of Buddha's chief disciples said:
*'Being in the forest with a complicated mind
is no better than being in a village or city with
a simple mind'*

Your brain receives instructions from your mind and you need an open mind to deal with change. You cannot cope with the process of life if your mind is closed and you are desperately clinging to the static, occupying yourself with the old, using old outdated knowledge. You are in control of your mind. Without uncluttering and emptying your mind of old garbage you cannot possibly accept or understand the new.

Closed minds do not inspire faith, courage or belief. A closed mind cannot see or listen because it is basically afraid, and even explanations do not help because the mind will only get more frightened. It is narrow and focused on its old habits, customs and traditions. Clear thinking and clear understanding go hand in hand. Opening the mind should not be a forcing process. By simply trying to approach everything with clear awareness the mind will open itself gradually.

In order to achieve a clear open mind you need to leave your thoughts alone and step out of them, so that you can look at them, observe and work with yourself, analyzing your thoughts and behavior. With persistence and practice you can acquire the attitude of the observer. Reading books on self development and/or attending workshops or seeking therapy always helps to get inspiration and to fill some gaps. Do not expect ready-made answers to be given to you on a platter. Use guidance and advice, by all means, but the actual work with yourself, you will have to do by yourself. Blind obedience to authority and becoming dependent on a teacher or a guru will do you more harm than good. Dependence deprives you of your will to strengthen your own intelligence and will rob you of your freedom. Do not accept what others say, nor reject it, but develop a curiosity to learn, to examine, to analyze and contemplate and only then make up your own mind. You can also take your time to make up your mind, do not allow anyone to rush you into any point of view or belief until you are ready.

Once you have made up your mind, do not worry about whether you are right or wrong, do what your feelings tell you to do, and it will always be right for you at that particular stage in your life. Remember your goal is keeping an open mind to change. An intelligent open mind is an agile mind that can move with direction. It moves with a purpose and is expansible. You must allow yourself to move, to flow with life, and you must do this wisely and intelligently. You can only do this by keeping your mind aware and attentive, free from old beliefs, free from stubbornness, frustrations and depressions. A strong mind does not suffer from boredom, anger, frustration or unhappiness. A strong mind has learned to drop all that is negative and detrimental. The Dalai Lama, a great student of the human mind said, 'since even wild animals can gradually be trained with patience, the human mind also can gradually be trained, step by step. With patience, you can come to know this through your own experience.'

You actually have the power to alter dramatically the way you think and act. Remember to fill your mind with good uplifting thoughts, positive, soothing, calm and pleasant thoughts. This helps you to keep an open, clear mind to see your way out of the endless problems that beset every human being. With an open mind, your listening will be receptive and intuitive wisdom will flow allowing you to accept the new.

## *Your Feelings —*

*Everyone you meet is your mirror.*
*A loving person lives in a loving world.*
*A hostile person lives in a hostile world.*

Your thoughts follow your feelings and there are only two types of feelings, pleasant and unpleasant and it is our choice which feeling we choose to have. If you are neutral or numb then you are missing out on life.

Usually, we either run away from, or push away, whatever causes unpleasant feelings in us. We can, instead, take our reaction into our own hands and change this. When we experience our various feelings we become more aware of them and as we gain in awareness we are able to act rather than to react. Feeling love, compassion, empathy, kindness, forgiveness, joy for others as well as for ourselves should all be a part of our feeling experiences. These are enriching feelings that allow us to grow. If these are lacking in us it is to our detriment and we suffer. We can work on ourselves though to experience and to develop these feelings.

Life cannot be lived fully unless it is lived with both your heart and your mind. If you live with your feelings only, you could be blocked by your emotions which can get out of control. If you are too emotional and this can be quite exhausting and frustrating, you will react to everything that happens to you without distance and objectivity. A certain word or gesture can trigger in you an automatic response. In a negative situation this response could be immediate anger, resentment or fear and you react like a machine. When you are aware, with an alert mind, however, and you take time to reflect you would not react blindly and get angry. You would have more understanding for the other person and be in control of the situation. Both your mind and your heart have to work simultaneously together for you to understand and be master of any situation, allowing you to act objectively.

Your feelings, by nature, contain both love and hate, both positive and negative. Unless you train your heart to enlarge the positive feelings of love, goodwill and friendship through daily exercise, you have no chance of experiencing the peaceful feeling which love naturally generates. A law of nature is that the more love you give, the more love you will have, to give. If you have nothing but loving feelings then you will feel safe and secure, totally at ease and nothing can sway you or take this peace from you. The feeling of love gives strength and security and your world will mirror this love back to you.

Compassion is an excellent starting point for love. Compassion comes when you realize your own suffering within yourself. Only then can you feel with another person. If you are able to look within yourself and recognize the feelings of dislike, regret, worry, fear, hate and resentment, then you realize that everyone is subject to the same feelings, then you can feel with others and have compassion for their problems. The more your heart is full of negative feelings such as fear, resentment or hate, the less room you have to feel compassion.

Compassion is different to pity. You can pity someone without feeling true compassion or understanding the extent of the suffering involved. Compassion is when you can actually feel the suffering of others as if it were your own. Strive to observe your feelings at all times while keeping an open mind.

## *Your Faith —*

*'Faith is the eternal elixir which gives life
power and action to the impulse of thought
and is the basis of all miracles and all
mysteries which cannot be analyzed by
the rules of science.' Napolean Hill.*

Faith is one of the most positive powerful human emotions. It is as powerful as love and sex. With faith you can literally move mountains. Napolean Hill also said: *'Faith is the basis for all miracles and all the mysteries which cannot be analyzed by science.'* The feeling of faith is the element that connects you to the Higher Forces.

*If you believe you will win, you will win.*

*If you believe you will fail, you will fail.*

It is important to harbor positive emotions and to eliminate the negative in you, because the positive mind is more receptive to faith. Take Ghandi, as an example, who using the power of faith transplanted into the minds of two hundred million people, an idea and influenced them to unite as one single body. He believed in them and they believed in him. Faith removes all limitations. It would behoove all parents as well as managers and teachers to keep this in mind, in order to get the most potential out of their children, employees and students.

Having faith with all your being, your thoughts coupled with your feelings gives you such power that you can achieve what you set out to achieve overcoming every obstacle along the way. Faith fueled with the energy of your emotions, which are the feeling portion of your thoughts, give your thoughts vitality, life and action making it possible for you to manifest whatever you desire in the physical material world. Faith is an element which, when mixed with desire creates a direct communication with your Higher Intelligence. Belief is a state of mind that can be developed, and in order to have belief it is essential to have an open mind. You can train yourself to have faith by repeating affirmations daily to yourself. The affirmations will gradually influence your thoughts and actions until they become a part of you. When making your affirmations of course it is necessary that you believe in what you are saying, both intellectually and emotionally. Repeating affirmations superficially off your head like a parrot, without concentration will not bring any positive results. You must be able to feel passionately the affirmations and desire them as you are saying them. To have belief in yourself and to have faith in a higher power that is waiting for you to call on whenever you choose, gives you inner peace and unwavering courage. It helps you to be centered and balanced, which are prerequisites to concentrating and focusing on your goal, accepting no defeat.

The key to open the door to change is to have deep genuine belief in yourself and belief in your ability to deal with whatever changes that may come your way. This belief gives you the inner strength you need to handle any adverse and stressful conditions in your life. When you have faith in yourself you will also have faith in others. The secret to all healthy relationships both private and business is genuine trust and belief in one another. Dealing with someone who trusts and believes in you automatically brings out the best in you and in the same way when you trust and have faith with whomever you deal with, you bring out the best in them.

There is a difference between wishing and being. Ready to receive and willing to do. Should you be someone who finds it difficult to trust or to have faith begin with a simple exercise. Make a habit to count at least four blessings every single day and to be thankful for what you have. More often than not, we take our blessings and good fortune for granted and we are ungrateful not appreciating that which we have always believing that others have it much better than we do. Exercise the feeling of being grateful for that which you have. Do this regularly without fail for two weeks, every morning and every evening, and observe your feelings and understanding.

One of my patients some years ago had one huge problem. He was lonely, wanted very much to get married and have a family but no matter how much he desired, it never happened. He was in his 40s and getting desperate. He walked around totally depressed, ill tempered and unhappy. He complained about everything and everybody. He found no meaning in his life and he had no goals. He came to me for help. The fact was that he was a handsome intelligent guy with a promising career and no financial problems. He was physically healthy and free to travel and to socialize. He had siblings, many nieces and nephews. When I suggested an exercise to him, to count ten blessings every morning and to be grateful, his quick response was to say that he had no blessings and therefore he had nothing to be grateful for. It took a long time for him to see that the problem was in his attitude and perception of life. He had a negative and ungrateful attitude and enjoyed wallowing in self-pity. He took everything good in his life for granted and wanted more without having to do anything for it. It was too much for him to read books on self-development or spirituality. He was too lazy to invest time and energy in changing his destructive bad habits. Everything I suggested to him was too much for him and besides he said that he had no time for such things. 'I work hard' he kept repeating 'and I get no rewards for my hard work, I don't believe there is a God and it is just not fair.' Everyone around me gets rewarded but not me! He was too blind to see that he was not prepared to make any effort for what he wanted. He refused to accept that women were running a mile away from him because of his negative attitude. He had no faith in himself and even less in God. He wanted this or that to come to him and was resentful and angry when he did not get what he wanted. Life gives us back what we invest in it, if we are not prepared to invest anything in life, how can we expect anything back? Can we expect to withdraw money from our bank account if we do not deposit any money in it? Being involved and living with enthusiasm is the least we can do when we wish for something, and having faith surely makes all the difference. This was one sad case because this guy just wanted to stay in his miserable myopic state of mind refusing to deal with change.

Everyone has something to be thankful for. Think of the simple realities that you take for granted. On a physical level which is the most important, be thankful that you can see, hear, smell. Be thankful that you have your health. Be thankful that you have an education, or can afford to eat whatever and whenever you want. Then go on to other material luxuries that you might be enjoying, of which the majority of the world population cannot even dream about. Be grateful you have someone to love or someone who loves and cares about you and this does not have to be a lover. Be thankful that you have nice neighbors, a good job, a good friend, a garden. If you make an effort to think hard enough, you will begin to understand how lucky you are and just how rich a life you have. Recognize and understand that you are blessed with so much goodness and take note of others who are less fortunate than yourself instead of being envious of those who have more. I personally wake up every morning thankful for another day of living. It's a good way to start the day. If we are not grateful for what we have, we cannot expect more good things to come to us.

*No gain comes unless effort is made.*

*Buddha*

# 9

# Seven Way Action Plan

For you to achieve a change in your outlook on life and your attitude leading to self-transformation there are some necessary steps to be taken. Nothing comes from nothing so you need to invest some time and effort. These simple guidelines are to be interpreted to suit your own needs and the outcome will be varied according to your own personal experiences and growth. You might achieve a quick positive change or you might think that you're not making any progress at all. On the contrary, you might find yourself getting even more confused, which would be a good sign because this would mean that you are changing your beliefs internally. You might find the process difficult or easy, you might feel encouraged or discouraged, it all depends on your circumstances, on your own perceptions and how you manage certain experiences. Whatever the temporary experience might be, be flexible and be patient with yourself. Above all do not give up easily.

Although you should be doing your own thinking and reflecting, experiencing your own feelings and being, you might have a great need to talk to someone every now and again. In this case, do so. Talk to someone whom you feel close to and trust. Talk to a counselor, a total stranger, a relative or a friend. Avoid, however, chatting constantly to your friends about every little experience you have good or bad. Avoid also being influenced by others, who although meaning well, might interfere or stop your process of growth, through envy or ignorance. Trust yourself and make your own choices. What you need, but not necessarily, is someone whom you can talk to rationally, openly and without reservations, whenever you have the need, as you are going through the emotional changes. I still believe a counselor or an experienced older wise person is the best. Nothing is as effective as spending time on your own, with yourself, reflecting on things. Keep in mind that it is you who has to weigh and analyze your thoughts and your actions. No one knows you as well as you know yourself, no one can feel your feelings for you and no one can think your thoughts for you. Sometimes it is the process of speaking about what bothers you that helps in clearing up your cluttered mind. Do not set any time limit for your progress as there are no time limits involved here. The process of self-analysis, self-understanding and self-growth is continuous and endless and differs for each one of us.

As you are going through this process, it is important to remember not to neglect your daily life routine, duties and responsibilities. Do not make the mistake as so many do, of using the exercise of self-discovery as an escape from daily responsibilities and physical realities. Somewhere in the process you might discover a strong urge to go away to a retreat to be on your own and to be with others going through the same process, to digest your experiences so far and also to prepare yourself for the next step forward. On the other hand you might never get this urge. There is no general rule or pattern every one of us is different, You do what you think is best for you and what feels right for you.

## *The Seven Step Action Plan—*

Know yourself
Develop yourself
Control your destiny
Be active
Be a possibility thinker
Free yourself of your chains
Now is your future

## I – Know Yourself

*Change cannot be achieved with intellect alone*

Someone said, the individual convinced against his will is of the same opinion still. In other words, you need to have your heart in harmony with your head and the will to change. You need to be open to the process of change, both emotionally and intellectually. If you are only emotionally willing, your intellect will limit your progress and if you are willing with your intellect alone, your feelings will block your progress. Either way, if there is no internal harmony all your attempts to change will be fruitless. No one can force you into anything. Or convince you of anything, unless you yourself are willing to allow the process to happen.

The first step of the seven-way action plan, is the first key. Not understanding and working on this first step would hinder you from moving forward. You need a) to discover and understand yourself, b) to accept who you really are with all your strengths and all your weaknesses and c) you need to love yourself and to have respect for who you are as you are.

To begin with, it helps to understand that you are made of several layers of 'I's. YOU are *matter* plus *Essence*. Without the breath of life, your physical body, the matter, which is the most perfect machine ever created, cannot function. No science has been able to invent a perfect copy of the physical human body. No science has been able to pump energy into a dead human body to bring it back to life to function with intelligence. No science has been able to put intelligence into any man-made machine. For example although a perfect copy of the human eye, has been invented as a machine and this eye machine can move and follow objects exactly as the human eye can, decipher between colors, sizes and shapes, it is unable to tell the scientists whether what it sees is beautiful or ugly, or whether it prefers one object to another, or whether it has any preference for any one color over another. It is incapable to interpret meaning or to give reason behind what it sees. In other words the man-made eye machine does not have will power, emotions, taste or preferences. It has no feelings, it merely stores information and when commanded reproduces mechanically the stored data. In exactly the same way, a computer is a copy of some of the functions of the human brain but remains without feelings or higher intelligence.

Think of your many contradictory thoughts, feelings and actions. Think how much of the real you, you keep hidden deep inside you and how little you actually reveal of yourself to the outside world. Think of your capacity for imagination. Think of your instinct for survival and for your instinct to better yourself. Think of that sixth sense, your intuition. If you are honest with yourself, you would admit, that you are a very complex being and even you yourself have difficulties in explaining your actions or understanding yourself. This is true for all of us. We are all complex beings and we all without exception, have several levels of 'I's, which we feel and live with, yet we generally know very little about. For our purpose here in this book, we will begin with the basics and concern ourselves with only four levels of our being.

## Center of Gravity

| | |
|---|---|
| 'I' – my **mental body**<br>*the thinking machine* | **my intellect**<br>- head |
| 'I' – my **feeling body**<br>*the emotional machine* | **my moods**<br>- chest<br>- solar plexus<br>*(middle part of the body)* |
| 'I' my **physical body**<br>*the moving machine* | **my instinct**<br>- back<br>- spinal cord<br>*(lower part of the body)* |
| 'I' **the Inner Self**<br>*the Master within* | **intelligence**<br>*in you and around you connected with the Universe.* |

Your are incapable to voice your thoughts, show your feelings nor take action, without your physical body. In the same way, in order to go through the process of evolution, on the physical plane, this inner 'self' which is intangible, yet a very real part of you needs your physical body. The inner 'self' needs to breathe through your body, it needs to express and manifest itself through your physical form. In one way, you can look at the inner self, as a prisoner in your physical form, at the same time, it is also around you. This is what is meant when you hear 'God is in you.' This 'inner self' is a part of God. This is also what is meant when you are told 'God is all over and knows everything you do.' The universal intelligence that is in and around all living beings, is a part of God, a part of the Universe, the Essence, connecting everything and everyone. That is why you are a part of the WHOLE and when you harm or hurt anything or anyone, you are in reality harming and hurting the self, yourself. This inner self, the part of which is in you needs to express itself on the physical level and does so through your individuality. This is a privilege given to you at birth. Furthermore, the 'inner self' will not impose itself on you. You have to invite it and allow it to manifest through you. You have the choice and freedom, to make use of this gift given to you at birth, the breath of life and to interpret and unfold it to manifest in your own world anyway you like.

Your physical body is preprogrammed to develop naturally as you grow older. Your organs, muscles, bones and nervous system function automatically as long as you give your body adequate food and drink, exercise and rest. The physical body needs to be cared for and the miracle is, up to a certain extent, even if you hurt yourself, your body has an in-born mechanism to heal itself, provided you allow it to do so. Without your body you would not have your physical senses and you would not have the power of thought or speech, or the ability to read and write. Stop for a moment right here and reflect on this miracle. The miracle of your physical body, its source, its multi functions and its total perfection. Reflect on this perfect machine, given life at the moment of conception, born into a perfect system of an existing perfect intelligent universe. Reflect on how this perfect machine automatically goes through the cycles of aging and death in exactly the same way as nature does. Ask yourself what happens to this breath of life that is withdrawn from the physical body at the moment of death, with all the knowledge and wisdom accumulated throughout one physical lifetime. Reflect on whether it was just an accident of nature that produced such perfect unique mathematical precision that makes up the universe or whether there is a Mighty Higher Power and Intelligence behind it all. Reflect on whether there is a deep mystical meaning after all to each minute living thing, serving its purpose, in the vast evolution process.

In order to maintain your physical body so that it can serve you well, you would have to care for it. You would eat a healthy diet, work and exercise regularly and you would get adequate sleep, allowing your body the rest it needs. It is, therefore, sensible and to your advantage if you look after your body and see that it remains healthy. If you, however, abuse yourself physically, with excessive or unhealthy eating habits, alcohol or drug consumption, you would be harming your body, limiting your physical functions and your further healthy physical development. Whichever way you deal with your body, does not stop your body to grow and change from the child physical form to an adult physical body. It would, however, determine your state of health.

Your mental body, which can also be called your thinking computer, on the other hand, does not develop in the same natural process as your physical body does. Your mental development, in your younger years, depends entirely on the environment you grow up in, your parents, your education and your teachers and in whatever ways they influence you. By the time you are a teenager, you will have been pretty much conditioned in the culture you grew up with. Sometime during your teenage years, and this varies with each one of us, according to the circumstances you grow up in, you might learn to take over the responsibility for your own thoughts. The degree of how much you allow yourself to be influenced will then depend entirely on you. The decision whether you want to develop yourself mentally or not will be yours. It depends on how much effort you put into exercising your mental powers, to grow and expand. The choice is yours. You will need to exert yourself mentally, acquire knowledge through reading, studying, observing, thinking and understanding. The development of your mental body is not a natural process and depends entirely on how much enthusiasm you have for life and curiosity for more knowledge.

A child who has been left alone, without the company of people or other children and without an education whatsoever, does not advance intellectually or emotionally the same as a child who has enjoyed a normal life span with family, friends and school. Both, however, grow physically to become adults. Mental growth and intelligence, an open flexible mind, has not necessarily to do with book knowledge. Although acquiring book knowledge is good, it has to do more with being mentally active constantly reflecting and contemplating on life itself and everything that we read and experience. It has to do with being awake and alert. This can be learnt. Being intellectual does not necessarily mean automatically being aware. It could very well be that one is an expert in one subject but totally closed and insensitive to everything else in life. As an example, you can compare a highly intellectual businessman with a farmer. It is quite possible to find a farmer who has not enjoyed a higher education but through life experience, working with nature, and self-reflection, is super intelligent and sensitive to the true issues of life. This farmer can be, therefore, far above the intellectual who has busily accumulated and acquired a multitude of business knowledge from books and theory, but has not experienced true life nor exercised independent thought and, therefore, remains limited as far as real life issues or people relationships are concerned.

In a similar manner, your emotional body is a reservoir of perceptions, experiences and conditioning according to the way you were treated as a child and the environment you grew up in. As with your mental body, there is a great capacity for emotional growth but this does not happen automatically as with your physical body.

It requires personal effort on your part, to work with your own feelings, understand your emotions, sort them out, digest and develop them, so that you can grow emotionally and mature in a healthy way. The process of growth for both your mental and emotional capacity is ongoing and endless and takes a whole lifetime. This is what is meant with 'no man is an island unto himself.' A human being needs other human beings in order to learn to develop and cultivate relationships, affections, communication skills, commitment, responsibility, giving, receiving, loving and so forth. You need the interaction with others in order to work with your own emotions. Any interaction, both positive and negative, with another human being gives us the opportunity to cultivate our feelings. Every experience in life both joyful and painful is nothing but a chance for us to learn, to grow, to ripen and to fine-tune our emotions. If you observe most people who have gone through a lot of genuine suffering in life are usually the most sensitive and the nicest down to earth people, no matter what background they come from. This brings us now to the 'I' the master within, the inner self.

The nature of the self and its relation to the Creator is a basic theme in Indian philosophy, the Upanishads. *'Concealed in the heart of all beings, is the Atman, the Spirit, the Self, smaller than the smallest atom, greater than the vast spaces. The man who surrenders his human will, leaves sorrow behind and beholds the glory of the Atman by the grace of the Creator.'* (Katha Upanishad.)

This 'inner self,' is a very real part of each one of us without exception, with one difference and that is, in some of us this Self is dormant and in others it is awake in varied degrees. The 'inner self' is an intangible substance that can neither be seen nor touched physically. To gain contact to your 'inner self' requires your three bodies, the physical, the emotional and the mental to be in total harmony. This explains the importance put on relaxation and meditation. It is through relaxation that you can reach a state of total harmony enabling you to establish contact with the 'inner self,' opening the door to another level of existence. Having your physical, emotional and mental bodies, blending together in harmony and guided by the Self enables you to be a centered being who operates on a higher level of consciousness, to contribute constructively to your world, family, friends, profession, society and the universe.

Unless the Self is awake, one could say that you are moving, working, playing, eating and drinking, automatically going through the motions, as if you were in deep waking sleep. You are operating like a human machine. As you go through the day, you invariably switch on your automatic pilot and you react instinctively to stimuli but not really aware of how or why. You experience this when you get home from work not remembering exactly driving yourself home. Or you shower and dress in a hurry in the morning and not actually remember having brushed your teeth. Or you might be speaking to someone very close to you without really listening to what is being said. You might say something but not remember having actually said it. Sometimes, you may ask, did I really say that? Did I really do that? Your thoughts are influenced by your perception of your life experiences and environment, and these thoughts dictate your behavior pattern. Your actions are automatic and are an expression of your thoughts.

Your emotions are being conditioned in a similar fashion. They run in all directions reacting through habit and instinct, according to which button is being pushed as you interact with people. You react with anger, joy, laughter, rudeness, sadness, hate, disgust or frustration, based on your previous emotional experiences, hurts and pleasures. Imagine as an example yourself as a computer, with software and a keyboard. Some of your software are your emotions and thoughts for example and your keyboard represents your senses. Through your senses, sight, hearing, touch, smell and taste your computer is actually being programmed around the clock, non-stop, even while you are asleep. Whether you are aware or not you are being constantly programmed. Negative as well as positive, intelligent and useless information, everything is being taken in by you ad stored in your software. Unless you are sorting out with awareness and filtering the input, the software of your thoughts and emotions is being filled with all the incoming information regardless of its quality. Now imagine the damage that is done when you expose yourself without awareness to negative useless senseless input. Imagine when you do not edit or sort out the input to have your own clear perception, your own individual thoughts and emotions, how your reactions are automatic, prefabricated, artificial and predetermined.

It is only through awareness of the Self that you can begin to take charge of your life by consciously controlling your centers. With this awareness, of who you are, where you are going and why, you are able to understand and have control over yourself, your thoughts and your emotions. Through awareness you can achieve higher goals in your life with less effort. Regardless of race, gender, religion or profession, some people discover the Self, at an early stage in life, while others make this discovery much later. For some the awareness of the Self is present at birth. There is no general rule and each one of us has to make our own individual, personal and intimate experience. No one can do it for you.

Let us take a car as an example. The car complete with engine and fuel is useless without a driver who has the knowledge of how to make it work. The driver who knows how to operate the car, however, is also useless and would drive the car in all and any direction, if he did not know exactly where he was going. In the same way, compare the car, to the human body, and engine and fuel, to man's energy and emotions, the driver who knows how to drive but does not know the destination, to the human being who uses his physical animal urges, intellect or emotions alone. Unguided by the inner Self man is lost in spite of his intellectual knowledge or instinct for survival. The man who is, however, guided by the inner Self perceives more than the physical reality visible to the naked eye. As another example, take those who are slaves of modern trends and media whether it makes sense to them or not. They buy whatever fashion dictates, they drink whatsoever is 'in' for the moment and they follow a general modern trend of the moment. Peers, the commercials and the media manipulate them. Many religions have through time been misinterpreted and aim only to manipulate people to blind obedience, discouraging freedom of thought and understanding.

Awareness of who you are, what you are doing, when and why you are doing is one key to activate the inner Self. Every one of us is born with this Self and it is always there waiting to be tapped and discovered. The methods of making this contact with the Self can vary. Meditation and relaxation techniques can help in the process. Concentration is a prerequisite to meditation. Reading self-help literature, psychology, religion or philosophy can help you understand the process. Fasting, solitude and silence are major keys to contact the inner Self. It is when your mind is clear, free of heavy food, alcohol, smoke or drugs, your thoughts still, your emotions at peace and in harmony with the world around you that you can make the contact. The Self will never force itself on you, you have to prepare yourself and be willing to take the first step. It is easy to recognize people who have this contact with the inner Self. They are usually in control, quiet, always friendly and emanate an inner calmness and peace which is contagious. Here is a story of someone whose Self within is awake and active:

*Janice was only 35 when her husband Tom of 40 suffered a stroke leaving the right side of his body totally paralyzed. Both were attractive, healthy, active, loved sports and had three fine kids. In one instant, due to circumstances beyond their control, their whole life changed. Tom had a stroke. The children took it very badly and it took them some time to adjust to this new situation. Janice showed great inner strength and dealt with the whole situation in an admirable way, that I often thought a movie should be made of their story, as an example for others. Her reaction and behavior were extraordinary. She never showed one moment of weakness. She never complained. She was a pillar of strength for her kids and her husband to lean on. She accepted their reality and immediately began to inform herself on everything that was available on the market connected to living with an invalid.*

*Janice took charge of the situation and turned the whole family in a new direction, remodeled their house to make it easier for Tom to move around in his wheelchair, so everyone in the family adapted, felt comfortable and secure including herself. Fifteen years later Tom is still there, much better, but still very helpless and dependent on Janice. They joke and laugh when he tries to eat and the spoon ends up in his ear instead of his mouth, but she insists with a lot of love that he try anyway to help himself. She helps him in between, of course, cuts his meat and so on, but she makes it clear, with much love and patience that he has got to help himself too. And he does more and more. I, as their friend, feel comfortable when I visit with them, and we all have a laugh when I present Tom with an up to date issue of Playboy magazine! His favorite magazine. My being at ease is only possible because of the casual atmosphere around them free of all tension or resentment at their bad luck and tragedy.*

The story could have been very different. Janice could have been a weak person, and she could have just thrown up the towel and left Tom in the hospital, the family could have broken up, she could have started another life with another healthy man. She could have turned to drugs or alcohol. She could have been totally incapable of taking charge and spent the rest of her life being resentful and wondering 'Why did it happen to me?' I believe that without this contact with the inner Self, and without her faith in a Higher Power (and they are not religious) Janice could have never been so strong. She rose to the test and she accepted her fate and that of her family and since she could not turn back the clock to what life had been for them, she accepted it as it is and decided to make the best out of it for them all. At the same time, a lot has to be said in favor of Tom as well, who is very much in touch with the inner Self too. He did not become angry, bitter or resentful, he accepted his fate as well with dignity and is still able to smile, even though his smile is lopsided because of him being paralyzed. He still has his sense of humor and displays a lot of courage.

This is a perfect example of the family accepting and adapting to a new situation forced on them through circumstances beyond their control. Janice overpowered fear, laziness, anxiety, loneliness, and all unnecessary negative limiting feelings. She was full of love and had faith in herself and in the family. Most important of all, she maintained a sense of humor in the most adverse of situations and was able to laugh together with Tom soon after he was home with his wheelchair.

Obviously it was not all as easy as it sounds for Janice or for Tom. It takes a lot of love, courage, effort and patience to take such a hard blow of fate and not to turn bitter. It also takes understanding and healthy reasoning to accept things as they are. What I mean to point out here is the fact that something from deep within gave them the strength to go on, the way they did. The

Self within is an endless well of love, wisdom, strength, courage and universal knowledge that we can always draw on, regardless of who and where we are.

Discover who you really are, understand yourself and your thoughts, why you behave the way you do, learn to accept yourself and above all learn to like and love yourself. Accept your weaknesses but do not dwell on them, make an effort instead to improve on them in any way you can. Focus instead on your strengths, recognize them as your assets and work with them, improving them to build up your self- confidence. Above all be always honest with yourself. Remember everyone has faults and weaknesses and no one is perfect. The more you cultivate your strengths the more your weaknesses will have to rest on a back seat. You need to know who you are truthfully, in order to accept yourself and you need to accept yourself as you are, in order to like yourself. Only then are you able to love yourself projecting this love automatically out to the world around you. Your world will in turn mirror this love back to you. The key here is love. With love in your heart you can literally overcome anything.

# When the Dime Drops —
## 'Satori' — Awareness

The Self is a part of you that always knows what is best for you and always gives you the right answer because it is connected with the universe, the source of infinite knowledge. Consider your 'inner self' as your best friend, and you will never suffer from loneliness.

I am sure you are familiar with the expression 'when the dime drops' or 'the penny has dropped.' Some refer to the same as 'when the mind clicks.' It is the feeling when we have an instant of clear thought. An awakening. We get a bright idea. We get a solution to a problem or we have an answer to a question. Most of the time this happens accidentally and with no effort on our part when without realizing it, we are naturally relaxed and in harmony. At this moment we are unknowingly allowing the Self to communicate with us. Sometimes, we act on these hunches and other times we ignore them. Try to be aware of the next time when the dime drops for you and act on it. The answer or the knowledge you get from the Self is always perfect.

Instead of leaving it up to chance waiting for the dime to drop, you can take matters into your own hands and make it happen for yourself whenever you need it. As a matter of fact you have the ability to go further and make it a regular part of your life. You can learn and practice to develop yourself to be in constant contact with the inner Self-introducing unity and harmony into your life.

## *Silence, Solitude and Sleep —*

Silence is golden, says an old proverb, universal and known to almost everyone. In total silence, without the sound of chatter or music, no book to occupy your intellect, no telephone or TV to distract you is an adventure of self-discovery. Sitting still or lying down and listening to the silence might be nerve racking when you begin but once you get accustomed to it, it is most calming and soothing to your nerves and psyche. With practice you can even enter the silence at will, where you can recharge yourself with whatever attributes you need.

Solitude is necessary so that you can gather your 'selves' together, to relax and to feel unity within yourself. Solitude is refreshing. Make a habit of spending some time alone, reading or listening to light calming music you enjoy, concentrating on a hobby or some hand work, alone with your thoughts. This can be quite refreshing.

Early to bed, early to rise makes a man healthy wealthy and wise, is another very true old famous proverb. Unfortunately, we ignore all this free good advice handed down to us from generation to generation and then we wonder why we are stressed, get ill and need therapists and psychologists. Going to bed before midnight, whenever possible does actually help you to have a quieter and more peaceful sleep and getting up early is a healthier beginning for the day. The average person feels good with eight hours of sleep but it is really up to you and whatever you feel good with. You should listen to your body and what it needs. Some people have enough rest with six hours or less and others might need ten hours or more. Too much sleep, however, can be just as unhealthy as too little sleep. The more hours you sleep, over and above the usual normal hours, the less energy you will have. If you need to sleep more than twelve hours on a regular basis, then you should see a doctor. If you want to sleep on and find it difficult to get out of bed you might be suffering from a depression and you should do something about that. It is paradox but the more active you are the less sleep you need. The longer you sleep over and above your basic need for rest, the less energy you have.

The thoughts you go to bed with determine not only the quality of your sleep but also your mood for the next day. If you go to bed full of anger and resentments, your sleep will be restless and you will wake up tired with the same negative feelings that you went to bed with. This way you keep yourself in an endless circle of negativity. Make a habit of having good happy peaceful thoughts before going off to sleep. Be thankful for whatever good experiences you had during the day and be thankful also for the bad experiences as they help to teach you something about yourself and about life. Look forward to another day tomorrow for more good experiences and for another opportunity to learn. Forgive anyone and everyone who has upset you, relax and go to sleep. There is nothing worse than going to bed angry and full of resentments or hate. Practice this every single day until it becomes a habit and you will be surprised how well you will be able to sleep.

## *EXERCISE*

### *Breathing—*

Breathing is not only essential to keep us alive, but also to keep us healthy and in harmony with the universe. How you breathe has a great effect on how healthy you are. The more tense and stressed you are the shallower and the faster you breathe. You can avoid tension by breathing correctly.

To relax in general always inhale, as deep down to your stomach as you can, slowly— then hold this breath inside for a few seconds— and then exhale as long and as slowly as you can until the whole breath is out again. Very often we tend to keep back some of the breath inside us which is what causes us to tense. This is unhealthy. Learn to concentrate and to exhale all your breath. As you exhale relax your muscles, especially your shoulders and let go. Repeat this three to seven times. Each time relaxing your body more and letting go. Your thoughts should always be focused on the breathing. After you have relaxed, go back to a softer regular normal breathing rhythm without extra effort, always remembering to hold a few seconds between each breath, which with practice should be your natural breathing rhythm. Now begin to focus your thoughts on whatever it is you want to achieve, sleep, energy, health, a vision or whatever else it is your aspire for yourself.

Make a habit of exercising your breathing at least once a day. Preferably mornings when you wake up and at night just before you drop off to sleep. When you find yourself in stress, stop a minute, put your right hand on your stomach and your left on your solar plexus, stand or sit and take three to six very deep very slow breaths, focus on breathing out longer and on relaxing your body. Try it, it works.

## *EXERCISE*

### *Fasting—*

All religions have special days for fasting but hardly any explain the real reason for this. My belief is that religions found ways to dictate to the people who in general were ignorant and unaware, some things that would be good for their general health. Fasting is good for your general health, it allows your body to take a rest, at the same time it helps you to take a step nearer to contact your inner Self. If your inner Self is repressed for too long not allowed to manifest, nature finds a way to force you to fast through illness.

There are various ways of fasting. To begin with, for example, you can be more aware of your diet. Try to have one day a week of light food, i.e. raw or steamed vegetables, fruits or salads. If this is not possible, try tea and toast, or soup and crackers. Once you are successful with this, try a juice day or herb tea day once a week. From there you can move on to fasting one whole day with water alone. This you can then increase to two or three days if you can do it without forcing yourself and feeling uncomfortable. Five days would be better since the stomach lining renews itself every five days.

Do not attempt to fast longer than that without first consulting with a doctor for guidance or perhaps joining a fasting group that is monitored by some professional person who can advice, help and encourage. Long fasting without professional guidance can be dangerous and detrimental to your health.

Fasting one day a week is a good way not only to give your stomach a rest, but it is good also to cleanse your body of toxins and it is one natural way to keep your weight under control. Fasting is healthy to keep a clear mind.

# *EXERCISE*

## *Meditation exercise for Self awareness —*

Choose a time and place most suitable to you. It must be quiet, clean, neat and comfortable. Make sure you will not be disturbed. To help you with your concentration light a candle or incense. A flower in a vase, a rose for example will do as well. Dress comfortably and stretch your body and your neck, relax your shoulders, before you begin with the meditation.

Sit on a chair with your spine straight to allow the energy to flow, both feet flat on the floor, with your hands on your knees or palms up on your thighs, whichever is more comfortable for you. You can if you prefer, sit on the floor, legs crossed, yoga style, with your back straight. Try, if you can, to do this every day at the same time in the same place. Energy is collected in the environment during meditation and this will help you to relax as you continue to do your exercises every day.

Begin the first week with five minutes. Fix your eyes on the candle, the incense stick or the flower and sit still. Allow your thoughts to come and go gently, without forcing anything or trying to control them. Just be. Extend the time to ten minutes the second week or third week, and by five minutes each following week or two until you reach the maximum of what time you can spare for this meditation exercise. Half an hour or one hour. If you cannot spare more than fifteen minutes, that is fine too. There is no fixed law. Do what feels good for you.

You can if you choose to, at any time, close your eyes, concentrate on the darkness and try to find a point of light in the dark. Feel your body. Do not try to control your thoughts or to force your thoughts to go blank. That would be counter-productive. Just relax and let it happen naturally. Be conscious of your breathing. Hear and feel yourself breathe. The first three breaths can be long, deep and forceful, especially the breathing out, to get the tension out of the body, and then settle down to a slower rhythm. Breathe with a regular rhythm that is comfortable for you, in and out with a pause in between each breath. Whatever thoughts come to you, allow them to come and let them pass by, and very gently try to focus again on your body and the darkness. It is important that you do not force yourself into doing or achieving anything. Just BE.

If you do this regularly every day, without losing your patience or expecting anything miraculous to happen, in a few weeks you will begin to feel a change within, you will feel a new inner strength. With practice you can even learn to meditate and to relax, even if only for a few minutes anywhere, no matter how noisy it is you will be able to withdraw and go within.

Observe how this regular meditation practice affects you. Whatever you experience keep to yourself, the less you speak about it the better for you. Your friends will notice the positive difference in you and will inevitably wonder. Let them. Don't feel obliged to explain anything.

## EXERCISE

## *For better Concentration —*

A good concentration power is a great asset for everyone because it influences everything that you do and enhances the quality of your life. Schools ought to make this a part of their curriculum for most of young people suffer from lack of concentration power and there is no reason for that because one can learn to develop the ability to concentrate. Here are a couple of easy examples.

To begin with, sit for ten minutes and concentrate on a task. Any task. Reading, writing, craft work, painting, pasting, gardening, it does not really matter what, the important thing is to concentrate on this one task and nothing else, in silence, without outside stimuli, i.e. music, radio or talk, for the whole predetermined period of time. Extend this by five minutes, daily or weekly depending on the task. Concentrate on nothing else but to do the task at hand well.

This exercise will train you to get involved and to relate to your task, focusing your attention with full concentration.

Another way to improve your concentration power is to sit still comfortably and concentrate on one object. Fix your eyes on and concentrate on the one object. Do this for 5 minutes regularly daily. Fix your whole attention on this one object without moving and without having your thoughts wondering off. Observe how you feel after each session.

You might think but this sounds easy. Believe me it is not as easy as it sounds for those who lack the ability to concentrate.

## II – Develop Yourself

*Knowledge and understanding are quite*
*different.*
*Only understanding can lead to being*
*Whereas knowledge is passing.*
*One must strive to understand.*
*Only by understanding can we reach God.*
Gurdjeff.

It is the birthright of every human being to be on the road of awakening, moving towards higher consciousness. Some of us are open to receive the messages life offers us while others develop less rapidly because they do not understand the messages not realizing that individual effort is necessary to develop further, or they are totally closed to the concept of self-improvement. No two human beings are alike, physically, emotionally, mentally and spiritually. Whatever we comprehend, in our innermost depths, as truth is always our own perception according to our own reality.

Let me explain. If you want to study to be a lawyer, an architect, a politician or a doctor, it is required that you attend university for a specific number of years. You have to study and pass exams before you can graduate and receive your diplomas. You are graded according to how well you answer the exam questions. Some study and others don't, some understand and some don't, some cheat and most don't. For whatever reason you get your grades and your diploma. Later you work in your profession, some might settle to do a mediocre job as long as a regular income is guaranteed. If you are ambitious and you want to be better than others, you make an extra effort, work harder and in time, with many years of practical experience, you become an expert in your field. How good you are and how much you advance depends entirely on how much effort you put into the process. It also depends on how well you actually understand the knowledge that you have acquired and whether you are able to put this knowledge to practical use. It also depends on how much energy, creativity and initiative you invest, and whether you continue educating yourself in your field in order to avoid stagnation. It works in exactly the same way with the development of the self. With one difference, you are not awarded any diplomas! As you develop yourself to a higher consciousness level, you discover your hidden potentials, and some of your many rewards will be inner strength and self-confidence. You will be a person of quality because you will have that little bit more to give into your profession. The more you work on yourself, the more harmony and success you will have both in your personal and professional life. The individual with a higher consciousness creates a peaceful world in which to live and this can be done regardless of whether or not you are with people who are consciously working on their growth. You are able to enjoy life on all levels, privately and professionally.

We are all equal and every one of us has the capacity for clear perception, growth, wisdom, peace and love. But unless we work consciously to achieve a higher level, the hidden splendor within will never manifest and we continue with our lives full of turmoil, fear, desperation and anxiety. We must remember that we are all fellow travelers on this road to awakening. The best teacher you can have is life itself, for you will find that you are always putting yourself into learning situations that are ideal for your growth. All you need to do is be open to receive and understand from the opportunities given to you, and you will find that life situations will make you aware of the exact inner work you should be doing.

I grew up in the Middle East and life at that time was much less hectic than it is now, giving me a lot of time to spend with myself in spite of the large family and the many activities going on.

I had grandparents, aunts, uncles and cousins around me of all ages and temperaments some of who were very wise. I learned something from them all. I also learned a lot from the many fairy tales that I heard everyday, which always carried hidden messages of wisdom. When I had a problem I knew exactly what to do, whom to go to, to talk about my problem. There was always someone around who would listen to my woes with love and understanding.

Unfortunately life today does now allow us this luxury, everyone is mostly stressed and too busy running from one thing to another, plus the fact that in most of our modern world we are not surrounded by close relatives whom we can trust, talk to intimately and share our problems. The older generations with the wisdom most of them have inevitably acquired throughout their lifetime, are often neither appreciated nor wanted. In some eastern cultures age is looked upon with respect and getting older means acquiring wisdom and dignity. The older generations play an important part in the family scene. Unfortunately the western culture has lost this, and getting old is looked at almost as a disease and one tries everything that modern technology and surgery can do to remain physically young. Forgetting that not only is it

131

hopeless to fight the course of nature, but that youthfulness, the same as beauty, comes from within. Youth and energy does not depend on how one looks but on how one feels, thinks and behaves. We are all very busy with our lives working hard so that we can earn enough money to buy all the gadgets and material luxuries which we cannot imagine living without. It is very hard to find a quiet place and a quiet moment so we can think about our experiences of the day, to digest what we have lived through and to contemplate on the most important issue of all, the true meaning of life.

Thoughts, experiences, emotions and knowledge have to be digested mentally and emotionally exactly the same way as the food you eat is digested physically. This can be done through reflecting on what you experience through solitude and silence. Observe your thoughts and behavior as you operate in your daily life. Contemplate over why you think the way you do and whether you feel comfortable with your thoughts. Acknowledge your thoughts even if they are negative and accept them as they are. Acknowledge and concentrate on your positive thoughts, expand on them, for it is the positive thoughts that comfort you and energize you, making you feel good. If you find yourself reacting to a situation with anger or annoyance, stop and ask yourself whether it is worth it for you to get so angry and to waste your energy in this way. Analyze your feelings, ask yourself why you are so angry and try to answer yourself truthfully. Anger is a negative emotion and will cost you energy that you could be put to better use positively elsewhere. Practice detachment by observing the whole situation with you playing a role as if it was a scene on a stage. This helps you to distance yourself and to have a more objective point of view.

As you seek guidance and help from books, therapists or seminars try not to be influenced by what you read or hear but make up your own thoughts and mind. Try to understand the information you are receiving and analyze it in connection with yourself and your experiences, and listen to your own feelings. It is a combination of heart as well as intellect that you are looking for. Responding with feelings alone would be too emotional and perhaps irrational; following your intellect alone to dictate your decisions might be too technical, cold and rigid. It is the golden middle line that you are looking for, of balancing intellect with emotions. It is the impulses you get from your intellect combined with your heart that you should always be open to. When in doubt follow the feeling in your solar plexus, your stomach, or as one says your 'gut' feeling. I usually combine my reason with my feelings but if ever I am in doubt and I find myself torn between the two, my intellect and my feelings, then for me there is no question, I follow my gut feeling. From my previous experiences I know that when I have followed my intellect, telling me clearly that this was the only logical thing to do, I ended up being extremely unhappy. When at a loss not knowing what to do, I end up with a stone in my stomach and a pain in my heart torn between what is logical and what my heart was trying to tell me which is illogical. I found out through pain and suffering, that for me the logical answer is not necessarily always the right answer.

You must discover what is right for you. With trial and error you will eventually find out what works best for you. Do not be disappointed or annoyed with yourself if things go wrong for you, which they are bound to every now and again, we all make mistakes and it is through our own mistakes that we learn best. Negative experiences are sometimes necessary for our growth. It is through developing yourself to a higher consciousness level, that you gain freedom of thought. This will help you to gain the confidence to dare to be different from others and not be afraid to speak your mind. Many people are sucked in to a group, a style, a way of thinking or certain behavior patterns, only because they are insecure and easily influenced by the media, peers, neighbors or society. Without awareness of ourselves we are reduced to being slaves to our own habits, following general trends dictated by markets. On the surface surrounded by all the material props, we might give the impression that we are living a quality life. However, when we scratch a little bit under the surface we might find nothing of real substance there and with the first signs of change that bring any type of problem, we are overwhelmed, we break down in pieces and are unable to handle the pressure. Let me tell you Renate and Walter's story:

*Renate, a therapist, in her thirties, was heartbroken when one day her boyfriend Walter informed her that he wanted to break up their three-year relationship. She was caught off guard because she felt that they had a very intimate and happy relationship. She knew that he suffered from depression every now and again and she always did her best to help him through these difficult periods. She was also aware that he was searching and looking for help from psychics, tarot card readers and astrologers. When, however, he came home one day and informed her that he must follow the*

135

*advice given to him by one psychic, to end all his personal relations, change his job and begin a new life somewhere else, she was not prepared. This was a shock for Renate who was a very sensitive, kind and loving person. There was nothing she could say to make him see that he should listen to his heart and make up his own mind, not just follow a tarot card reader's advice on what he should be doing with his life.*

*Rather than search within himself Walter was desperately looking for answers for his dissatisfaction outside of himself. Needless to say any relief he might find would only be short lived and the only way to find peace was to look into himself inwardly. This he could only do if he took time to spend with himself and the courage to face his feelings of inner confusion. In looking for an answer to his problems through others, he was running away from facing himself, refusing to accept his most inner true feelings, whatever these might be. He refused to take responsibility for himself.*

*Walter might be hiding a part of himself. Perhaps he was hiding feelings and desires deep within which he was incapable of showing or sharing with others. Perhaps he was pretending to be someone he was not in order to be accepted by society. Perhaps he was living a life and working in an environment he did not enjoy, and in reality did not want, but was forced into because of family or peer pressure. There could be several reasons for Walter being unhappy. The tarot card reader might have been right and she might have told him what he wanted to hear. But he preferred to push the responsibility on her rather than to admit the truth and to say honestly to his girlfriend 'this is what I want to do.' Anything is possible we don't know only Walter knows.*

*The true answer and the right solutions Walter can only find for himself through the journey of self-discovery. Granted this would be a more difficult path to take than to seek refuge in a comfortable and convenient solution. Walter might get lucky and might get advice from someone who will lead him on the right path to make his inward journey. He might stumble on the truth sometime or may be not at all. One thing we know for certain and that is that no one can force him to face himself. He must take that important first step alone.* As it says in the Bible: *'Knock and it shall be opened unto you and 'Seek and ye shall find.'* If you make a personal effort and you ask for help or support, doors will open for you. It is that simple. If you make an effort to search you will find what you are looking for. Nothing will happen for you, unless, you make the effort first. Develop the habit of giving before asking and without expecting something in return. Believe it or not your rewards will be greater. Sometimes your rewards come to you unexpectedly and indirectly when you least expect them.

In the business world individuals led by the urge to make maximum profits, put much emphasis on the development of managerial skills, marketing or sales techniques. This is fine if the people concerned have a developed self and have the ability to understand and to use these new acquired business techniques constructively and for the benefit of all concerned. Unfortunately, however, more often than not, the information is acquired hungrily and accumulated quickly externally. This is then used without any understanding, sensitivity or intelligence and with only one goal in mind, to satisfy the personal ego and for the benefit and profit for the individual or organization, at the expense of all else. In the same way too much emphasis and importance is put on university and professional degrees giving the degree holders entry into fields and positions far beyond their competence. Also in this case the self-development aspect is neglected and the most important of all the digesting and understanding of the material consumed combined with real life experience is missing. Too much weight on data and too little or non at all on the human aspect which is really the most significant no matter what field we are talking about. It is paradox that we are living in the era of communication and yet the majority of civilized mankind suffer from isolation and loneliness. People in general are finding it difficult to communicate; it is as if everyone is speaking a different language.

**EXERCISE**

## *Ways to Self Growth —*

— Acquire a habit to read at least one book every month or two on modern psychology, philosophy, religion or self-growth. Make notes of points that are of particular interest to you and which you might like to refer back to at a later date. We need healthy mental food regularly, exactly in the same way that we need healthy food for our body.

— Acquire a habit to listen to classical music or any other music of your choice, as long as it is relaxing and soothing. Music is a universal language and through sound vibrations can expand your mental and emotional state of being. There are many books on the market of how music and sound affects your mood and your psyche. Certain music is soothing and relaxing, other music is energizing. Music can awaken aggressiveness and violence in you, on the other hand, it can relax you and make you peaceful. Music can also make you creative and energetic.

— Colors have the same effect on your mood and psyche. You are influenced by the colors you surround yourself with. The most peaceful are naturally pastel rainbow colors. It would be very difficult to sleep peacefully in a red room for example, you would never see a red or black hospital room but you would see a red or black bedroom where sex is priority. There are many books available on the market on color therapy. Inform yourself about this, so that you can understand this field better, for your own well being and especially if you have young children.

— Another good source to learn about life is to spend some time with older people. Let them do the talking and you do the listening. If you are lucky and you have a large family with grandparents, uncles or aunts, this is your chance. If you do not have close family members, then adopt a grandparent from the neighborhood, go out regularly for walks or visit with them. This way you would be doing them and yourself a favor. This good deed will make you feel good about yourself.

— Last but not least I again stress the importance to spend time regularly with yourself in silence and solitude. If your life is such that you find it impossible to be alone every day, try then to spend a couple of hours alone once a week. You need to think about, to reflect and to digest all of your activities, to allow the experiences and the knowledge you have accumulated to sink in. You need to understand. This can only be done when you are alone.

— Open your heart and expand your horizon. Expose yourself to other cultures by traveling or by making friends with people who are different to you. Be free of prejudice and be interested in learning about their habits and their ways of thinking. We are all a part of a whole, inter-dependent more than we realize and should be supportive of each other. Our goal should be the well being of all mankind. We can each begin to contribute by practicing open mindedness and tolerance with our immediate family members and friends. It does not make sense if you are open and tolerant with strangers but closed and unfriendly towards your own family.

A good example to use here is this one: Imagine the world with all humanity of all races and color, the animal and plant world included with each part of the whole playing an important role in the whole mysterious existence of the universe. In the same way now imagine your body with all its various parts, nervous system, organs, limbs and senses. Now imagine a part or more of your physical body declaring war on the rest of your body, refusing to cooperate. Imagine precisely your left leg wanting to be independent and wanting to go in a different direction than your right leg. It sounds silly but imagine this for a second. Impossible right? Or imagine something more possible, your stomach refusing to digest the food you eat, how do you feel, can you work or sleep then? What would happen to you as a whole? If any cell or organ in your body does not function properly and does not contribute what it should to keep the body healthy, you are immediately ill. It is exactly the same with the world we live in. Human, mineral, animal and plant kingdoms are all of the same significance. All humanity regardless of race or color must cooperate and live together in harmony for each human is like a small tiny cell contributing towards the whole universe and is, therefore, of equal importance.

Instead of complaining about what others do, accept responsibility first for your own thoughts and daily actions in your own world. Take responsibility for all of your thoughts and all of your actions. Instead of criticizing others observe yourself first and set a good example for others. If we all did this and concentrated on our own immediate world, the ripple effect out to the world would be positive and more constructive.

## *III – Control Your Destiny*

*Control your own destiny or someone else will.*
*Be pro-active and not re-active.*
*Accept responsibility for yourself.*

One of the most difficult tasks in life is to take responsibility for yourself. Responsibility is also an important step towards being in touch with your Inner Self. As children we are totally dependent on our parents and at some stage or another, some of us are able to take this giant step into independence and assume responsibility for ourselves. Others, however, never seem to be able to take this step and in adulthood they shift their total dependence from their parents on to their partners.

Accepting responsibility for yourself means you are independent in your thoughts and your actions. Your thoughts and your actions are based on your own conclusions after observing and perceiving a situation, making your own decisions and accepting the consequences. You do not depend on other people's opinion nor do you blame others if something goes wrong. By accepting full responsibility for yourself, you have agreed to carry a big burden on your shoulders, and if you are not accustomed to taking responsibility this could be quite frightening.

But then let's look at the other side of the coin. Taking responsibility for yourself also means freedom. It means freedom of thought, freedom of action, freedom for you to grow, to expand, and freedom to discover who you are. Freedom to turn around any pain or negative experience to your advantage by making it into a learning experience. Freedom to make 'lemonade' out of the 'sour lemons' you get in your life, as someone said. Freedom to be who you are. In other words responsibility can be very enriching. You are in control of your life. You are in control of your destiny. When you are in control, you are sitting in the driver's seat and you can go anywhere you please. No one can stop you. Accepting responsibility for your own life is a giant step towards gaining self-confidence and moving towards a higher consciousness level.

Once you have acknowledged and accepted the fact that so far you have avoided taking on any responsibility, and that you have the desire to change this, you have actually accomplished the first step in the right direction. Next you make a commitment to yourself that you will do whatever is needed to work on yourself and to learn. Then you observe yourself, analyze yourself, what you do and how you do it. Observe your thoughts, your feelings and your actions. Analyze your relationships and make a list of any decisions made, even if it is a trivial decision such as drinking a cup of coffee. Which decisions do you make for yourself and which decisions are made for you, make notes as you go on. Writing things down has the effect of bringing it home to you very clearly. Once it is written down you have to face it. Thoughts can be pushed aside and excuses found and forgotten too easily. Whereas when you see it on paper, you cannot deny it and you have to accept it as your reality.

It is always fine to ask other people for their opinion, but try to stay true to your own self and listen to what your own feelings tell you. Digest all the information you hear, and come up with your own version of how you understand it, find your own answers and make your own decisions. Making a wrong decision is better than making no decision at all and even if you make a bad decision, which no doubt you will sometimes, remember that there is always a lesson to be derived from your bad experiences. You can get inspiration if you wish from visiting workshops, reading books on self-improvement or you can learn by observing others in action. It does not really matter what you do as long as you make up your own mind arriving to your own conclusions weighing every alternative that is available to you.

A good way to practice taking responsibility for yourself is to take very small decisions on a daily basis and to keep this up religiously. Every night before you go to sleep, you decide on something that you want to do the day after. The next day you make sure that you carry this decision out, exactly the way you had decided. For example, you decide, tomorrow, I am going to wear my blue suit with a specific blouse, or tie and shoes, etc. Or, tomorrow, I am going to call my friend, someone you have been meaning to call for a long time and never got round to it, or, tomorrow I am going to exercise for ten minutes, or write a letter, etc. It does not matter what the decision is, as long as it is some small constructive task that you need to do and that you can easily do. The idea is not to make it too hard for yourself. What is more important is that you carry our your decision daily without fail. After practicing this daily for a few weeks, you will begin to experience self-satisfaction and a sense of having accomplished a goal. What you will achieve with this exercise is practicing concentration and discipline. You can go on from there in the same way to bigger decisions repeating the same procedure exactly.

If you have a decision of a much larger dimension to make, try the following: You make a list on paper and this is very important, of all the possible solutions that come to your mind. Logical or not, even if it seems impossible, write down what comes to your mind. The idea is not to limit yourself to only what you believe is possible. Often we immediately rule out what we perceive as impossible, limiting our views and options. Instead be creative, daring and adventurous and let your imagination go. You might just find out that what you perceived to be impossible is not that impossible after all. This is when you open the door to the possibility of miracles. Next you write down next to each solution what the outcome could be and what could possibly go wrong. This exercise of writing down the solutions in detail and the risks involved weighing the alternatives available to you, is a great tool in helping you to make a decision on any important issue in your life.

One other way to find a solution to a major crisis is for you to go for walks alone. While you walk try not to think about your problem. Instead look at nature around you, concentrate on the sky, the birds, trees etc. and you find that as you walk in the fresh air, breathing deep and quietly on your own, being in tune with nature, an answer will cone to you loud and clear. The importance of the fresh air and being alone is to relax you so that you are in harmony and open to receive clear messages from your Higher Self and the Universe.

An age-old remedy to sleep over your problem works too. Sleeping over your problem does not mean your worrying yourself sick over it, being tense and cramped and staying awake all night tossing and turning unable to sleep. This is what you do instead, you go to bed with a clear head, not having had alcohol or sedatives, read a light book if you must to take your mind off your problem. Then you lie in bed, be aware of the problem you relax your body, then hand the problem over consciously to the Self and ask it silently to find the solution and to make it clear as to what you should do when you wake up in the morning. Then release your problem, forget it, let it go. Now have faith, relax and sleep peacefully. Your inner Self will do as you asked. Repeat this every night until you have found your answer. It is important to remember not to continuously worry or speak about the problem during the day. Worry and stress stops the energy flow blocking you from receiving any message from the Self. Speaking and complaining about the problem will only feed it more negative energy and make the problem grow.

On the other hand, should you have a problem and you do nothing to try to solve it, then in a way you have also made a decision in that you have decided to remain passive and let things be as they are. You must then take responsibility for having made the decision not to take any action. In this case you cannot make excuses or shift the blame on to someone else when things go from bad to worse and they will because when things stagnate they inevitably go from bad to worse. You have no one but yourself to blame because it was your own decision to remain passive and not to take any action. Classical examples are, those who feel trapped in a job or in a marriage and complain about it every day, but do nothing to change the situation, because of a million reasons and then say innocently '...but I didn't do anything....' and that is where the problem is exactly. They did nothing to remedy the situation. They chose to remain passive and made no effort to rectify a bad situation. Passivity can be damaging too.

Many people are in the habit of blaming everyone else for their misfortunes in life. They themselves are never to blame for anything that goes wrong for them. Such people seem to enjoy playing the role of the victim. The 'poor me' 'pity me' role. It has always amazed me to listen to adult men and women in their forties or older, blaming their mistakes in life on to their parents, especially their mothers. Those poor mothers who seem always to get the blame for everything while the fathers are very conveniently absent. Here is an example:

*Peter was in his forties. He had immigrated to the States in his thirties and was determined to lose his German identity and be an American in every way. He was full of hate and resentment towards his mother whom he often spoke about, blaming her for many terrible things that had happened to him. The sad thing was that his mother had died when he was twenty. This was in the seventies and everyone in New York was on a trip of self-discovery and Peter was no different. Following the advice of teachers an gurus, he gave up all his material belongings, changed his name and was all set with a new found self, in his own words, like a new born baby, to begin a new life.*

*Having dinner with him one evening, I listened as he told me with much excitement about his new identity, new self and new found happiness. After a few glasses of wine, his mother crept into the conversation and I could see his resentment and hate creeping up on him taking hold of him. I listened to him a little while and then I asked him how long has it been since his mother died. He said: 'Oh, it's been twenty six years.' So I said: ' Peter, don't you think it's time that you let go of your mother and let the poor woman's soul rest in peace. After all you are an adult and you have been responsible for your own life for the past twenty six years.' It was at this moment that something clicked in his mind. One remark, which could have been from anyone, at the right moment, because he was receptive, did it for Peter. He realized in a flash that he had never emotionally let go of his mother. He understood in the same instance that it was time for him to take responsibility for his own thoughts and actions. In one flash he saw how ridiculous he was, a man of forty six, complaining about and blaming his mother, dead for more than half of his life, for all his mistakes and unhappiness. I saw all that in his face in one instant.*

All the years and years of searching, workshops, reading books, Gurus, identity change and giving up all material possessions, must have done something for him I presume, to get him to the point where he was now at this dinner. However, I wonder if it was really necessary that he go through a complete identity change including his name and giving up everything material that he owned right down to his last shirt. Who can say, it takes all kinds of experiences for people to finally see through their problems clearly and to find their own way to happiness. Perhaps Peter needed to go through all these experiences before he was ready for that one moment when the dime finally dropped for him. Soon after, I heard that Peter got married and moved over to Hawaii and hopefully to live happily ever after!

Let's look at another example:

*Gertrud and Horst were married for twenty five years. One fine day, when all the kids had left home, Horst informed Gertrud that he was leaving her. Obviously they had been having problems but she never really thought he would go because it never occurred to her to leave him. Naturally she was stunned. Gertrud refused a divorce. Now after ten years of separation Gertrud is still refusing to let go.*

*She insists on living in their big house all alone. Horst is not wealthy and has a problem in maintaining the huge house where Gertrud lives now alone plus maintaining his own new home with his girlfriend whom he loves and wants to marry. Gertrud is unable to or does not want to contribute to make it easier for him. So the emotional pressure is even greater because of the extra financial stress that they both have to deal with. Naturally the children feel sorry for her, she is their mother after all, but they also understand their father and why he left. Gertrud is a negative person by nature, she is lazy, does not exert herself to do anything that requires effort and complains continuously about Horst being a jerk for walking out on her and breaking up the family. She's only fifty-five and has at least twenty years more to go if not more. The way things look right now she will be doing exactly the same thing in twenty years. Unless she falls ill that is, which she is very likely to do. She enjoys being miserable and enjoys playing the victim game. She refuses to take her life into her own hands and to accept responsibility for herself and her actions. She is blocking her own growth and limiting herself to her meaningless unhappy existence.*

*The children have stopped going home that often because it hurts them to see their mother like this, but she does not seem to realize this. No matter how much they try to talk to her, to help her, her mind is shut tight and she refuses to listen. Unfortunately, it seems as if only a catastrophe of some sort could force Gertrud to wake up from her deep miserable sleep. This is a typical case where a person is neither acknowledging nor accepting the inevitable, which means letting go so as to move on to gain other experiences and grow.*

By stagnating and blocking the flow of things, she is not only harming everyone else involved, but herself most of all. At this point, nothing should be more important for her than to look towards the future, pick up the pieces and whatever it takes to begin afresh again. No one can do it for her, she has to take the first step herself. The longer she procrastinates, the older and the more difficult she will be, and the more difficult it will be for her to change her life style.

The story of Horst and Gertrud is not unique. Many hang on suffering in unhappy relationships due to financial or emotional dependency but fear of change is the most common I would say for refusing to let go.

## *EXERCISE*

## *Relaxation before going to sleep—*

Not many people realize that one has to prepare oneself for a good night's rest, just the same as when one prepares oneself in the morning to face the day. If you take your time and do this without rushing and aware of your every move, you will find that both your day activities and your night sleep will be more meaningful and rewarding.

Having washed yourself, brushed your teeth and hair, wearing a loose nightgown or pajama, make yourself comfortable in bed. Your room should be tidy and clean, the air fresh. If you can sleep with a window open slightly, do so. Fresh air helps you to sleep better. Making a habit of going to bed early and waking up early is to your advantage. Lighting a candle, or incense and listening to soft slow relaxing music while preparing yourself for bed also helps. All of these preparations or some at least, are important to relax you to have a good night's sleep. Turn off the music and light and get into bed.

Once you are lying in bed, stretch and settle down comfortably. Contemplate your day; get rid of any negative feelings, such as jealousy, envy, anger, hate, worry or resentments. You cannot enjoy peaceful and restful sleep if you are tense and blocked with negativity. Stretch your body, wiggle your toes, relax your neck, settle down and close your eyes. Take a couple of deep slow breaths looking forward to a good night's sleep and to waking up fresh in the morning.

Settle down to a relaxed slow breathing rhythm, remembering that breathing out is just as important as breathing in. Beginning with your toes and legs you move up in your mind, willing silently your body to relax. Move very slowly up your legs and thighs to your hips, relax all the way, then keep moving up slowly to your waist, your solar plexus and your chest, always aware of your breath, breathing softly. Now move your focus on to your fingers in both hands and move up your arms very gently and slowly relaxing them all the way up to your shoulders. Now concentrate on your shoulders and neck relaxing them, then your facial muscles and your head. Your last thought before dozing off should be to ask the Higher Self to be with you the next day when you wake up in the morning. All of this ritual has a calming effect on you and your psyche as your are focusing on relaxing yourself.

If you have a problem and are looking for a solution this is a good time now to ask your Higher Self to help you find a solution and to show you this clearly. Repeat this exercise every night, before going to sleep ad ask for help if you need it, until you have your solution. You will be surprised how well you are able to sleep and how easy solutions will come to you. In return, promise to do one small deed each day and remember to keep your promise. The deed can be something very simple such as being friendly to someone you dislike. Or making someone happy by giving them a flower, buying them a cup of coffee, calling your mother or father, or doing an extra favor to someone who really needs it. The idea is that you make an effort to make someone else happy without expecting something in return. A selfless act. There is a good reason for this, it will not only make someone else happy but it will give you a sense of well being too. Try it out and see how good it makes you feel to be good to someone else without expecting anything in return.

On waking up in the morning and before you jump out of bed, remember to take a couple of deep slow breaths, take a few moments to collect yourself together, be aware of your thoughts, your emotions, your body and then slowly get up. You will find that you will carry this peace with you throughout your day.

## IV – Be Active and Effective

*Whatever you can do, or dream you can do*
*begin it.*
*Boldness has genius, power and magic in it.*
Goethe

*The balance of trinity -*
*8 hours of service, 8 hours of recreation and 8*
*hours of rest.*

Action is movement and movement is energy in action. Your energy level determines your activity level and at the same time, it is your level of activity that influences your energy level. In other words, the less you move the less energy you have. Movement is spiritual. The word spiritual refers to the evolutionary process, as it drives man forward from one range of sensitivity and responsiveness to outside influences, to another range. Movement and action lead to expansion of consciousness. The awakening and growing infant; the development of the wo/man into a sound and effective business wo/man; or any positive activity for that matter, that drives the human being forward towards some form of development, be that physical, emotional or mental is spiritual and is in accordance with the law of nature.

This is easy to prove. Take a week off and be as lazy as you can be. Sleep as long as you like, eat as much as you like and don't strain yourself to be active. Sit around, read a magazine or watch TV. Keep up this lazy 'dolce fa niente' routine for a few weeks. You might enjoy the first day or two, but soon you will feel yourself getting lazier every day, having less and less energy, boredom will inevitably take over, your motivation will disappear and after a longer existence in the same routine depression will surely set in.

This is an extreme example, but imagine a normal person instead. Peter for example, who has a normal life, with a job and family, going through a monotonous existence with a daily routine that does not include any sense of awareness, or balanced healthy activities to energize him or his family. To the outside world they seem like a perfect steady family. However, day after day, month after month, and year after year, living this uneventful life, Peter and his family often suffer from illness, depression, anger and frustration. They have all become slaves of their habits over the years and they feel drained of energy and vitality. Both Peter and his wife accept this as the normal state of being and are not only unwilling to change things but will not even consider it afraid of the unknown.

*In comparison let us now look at the life of Carlos, who lives with awareness and is in control of his life. Carlos is thirty, unattached and is concentrating on his career. He understands himself and he knows what he wants. Carlos likes to have a steady existence and dislikes taking risks. He takes pride and joy in himself and his life. He does everything in moderation, he sleeps adequately, and is not a workaholic but he puts in a few extra hours when necessary, because his career is important to him. He takes time for his physical well being, he walks, plays tennis, swims and attends Judo classes regularly. He has a few close friends and occasionally spends time with them. He does a lot of reading to keep up his knowledge of general politics and business activities. Carlos also visits a night school to earn a higher degree, which he needs in order to advance in his career. This of course involves many hours spent in school as well as studying. Believe it or not, Carlos also has a very warm and close relationship with his mother, brother and the rest of his family. Now you may think that this sounds unreal, how does Carlos get all this time and energy to do all these things, you might ask.*

For someone who is as energetic and motivated as Carlos is this is no secret. For others, however, this might seem impossible. But the truth is, it is possible.

Let me explain. First of all Carlos knows and accepts himself as he is. He knows what he wants, he has a goal and is, therefore, motivated. Motivation is energizing. Next Carlos has figured out a good plan how to make the best use of his time. He uses his time and energy effectively. By taking time for his physical activities, he makes sure that he is re-energized continuously. By taking time for his walks, he not only makes sure that he gets plenty of fresh air but also gets some time to spend in solitude with his own thoughts. To strengthen his will power and discipline, he practices Judo. For his emotional well being he makes an effort to spend time with his friends and to have a warm relationship with his family. His family is important for him because he is aware that this is a source of energy, support and security for him. The time and love he gives them is reciprocated and this makes his family feel good as well as himself. Whatever makes you feel good energizes you.

Carlos is also willing to accept the consequences. Some of the sacrifices might be that he has no girlfriend, or no sports car, or he has no time to hang around in bars or late night discos. You might be wondering if he is missing out on life, as perhaps many of his colleagues might think. The answer is no, he is not, because Carlos is doing what he wants to do, he has made his choice and he is fully aware of the consequences. He accepts the fact that he cannot have everything and he made his choices. It is his choice to be alone and to spend his evenings in school. It is his preference to spend his money on education rather than a sports car. He knows that nothing lasts forever and that in two years when his studies are over, he will have more time and money for other activities. He knows what his priorities are in life. Carlos has set himself a goal and he focuses his energy with awareness. He is using his energy constructively and effectively.

Let us imagine a situation where fate might give Carlos a hard blow and his circumstances change. Would Carlos break down totally, we wonder. I personally do not think so, because it seems to me that Carlos is the type of person who will be able to deal with unforeseen changes that are imposed upon him and he will rise to the occasion. He is accustomed to living his life in a positive and productive manner, he seems to have the inner strength and confidence and this will carry him through the rough periods in his life. Remember the energy you have at your disposal is neutral and it is your choice how you make use of this energy, there are always only two ways to choose from. You can choose to be negative and destructive or you can choose to be positive and constructive.

Be active physically, mentally, emotionally and spiritually because harmony and balance is the law of Nature. Occupy your mind with constructive activity to keep it off any physical or emotional hurt that you suffer, with your mind occupied you forget your pain. Be active to keep your body slim and subtle. Exercise, walk, play sports, swim or run. Be mentally active, exercise your mind to keep it young and fit. Being active will keep you popular with your family and friends. Inactive or passive people are boring and generally not very popular. When you are actively involved you are a happy person, and you also, inevitably gain and generate more energy and vitality. Energy and vitality give you sex appeal.

Be involved and genuinely interested when you communicate with people whomever they may be, in particular with your immediate partner and family. Focus on the person you are with, listen to what is being said to you attentively. People will feel your interest in them and will be drawn to you. Active people are generally youthful, healthy and interesting. They are always energetic and enthusiastic about life. I personally know people who are sixty years of age and older who look and behave ten or twenty years younger than their age, at the same time, I know young people in their twenties and thirties who look and behave ten years older or more than their actual age. Usually the company of the youthful and the active, regardless of age, is much more stimulating, inspiring and is more desirable. The company of those who are stubborn, who stagnate and who have a narrow vision is draining and tiring. Even younger people when lazy and inactive, can have this effect. When we are with someone who is energetic, enthusiastic and active, not only are we re-energized and re-charged so also is the other person.

When next you are with people, be aware of your own feelings as you leave them. Do you feel you want to be with them more often and go away feeling fresh and happy? Or do you feel drained, tired and glad to get away from them? Whom do you look forward to see? Avoid people who sap your energy.

Keep growing, expanding yourself and your horizon. The more you do, the more you will achieve and the more you achieve the more energy you will have. You can do this with your physical body, with your mental body and you can do the same with your emotions. Your physical body through physical exercises, your mind through mental exercise and training both in business and general knowledge. You can also keep your emotions active and growing through your different relationships, with your family and loved ones, with your neighbors and colleagues by analyzing your emotions and working on yourself, while you are relating with the world around you. Through attention and concentration you focus your energy by your action. Your actions are based on knowing who you are, what your values are and what is important to you, when you have a goal then you have a sense of direction. It would be difficult for you to know which direction to follow if you have no idea where you are going. The more awareness you have of the existing alternatives, the more likely your ability will be to consider any situation in its proper perspective before you take action.

An active person does more than think or talk. There is a difference between thinking and doing, so do not limit yourself to thoughts only. Activate your understanding. Ideas and information are like food, they must be eaten and digested mentally even if they don't suit you, and even if they cause you nausea. Mental activity keeps your mind young and agile because your brain muscles are the same as your body muscles. It is also important to use your eyesight actively, to see is passive, but to really look and understand what you look at, is active. Nothing in the world can touch you, limit you, or harm you, save that which acts through your own feeling world, your emotions.

Everything that you do counts the positive as well as the negative. Since there is constant movement, either forward or backward, nothing is really neutral. So if you are standing still, and everything else is moving forward around you, then you are in fact being left behind and therefore moving backwards. It takes a tremendous amount of effort and energy to deal with change if you are at a stand still and left far behind. Imagine yourself taking part in a race, and all the runners take off and you are just standing there. The nearer the runners are to the goal, the further they are from you, and in comparison with them you are further and further away from the goal. The longer you delay your start the longer it will take you to catch up with them.

As you keep yourself active make sure you are effective, involved with positive action and constructive. I.e. Learning, creating, giving, sharing, serving etc. Reflect on your actions. As you continue to be constructively active, you find that you will have less and less time to be idle, to be involved with gossip, or to harbor negative thoughts such as hate, envy, jealousy, anger or fear. Your thoughts are occupied, instead, with your activities and you have no time and no room for destructive thoughts or behavior.

At a workshop I was giving, a housewife asked me if it was possible to live a life without being involved in gossip. The answer was yes, it is. Gossip is not only empty and harmful but a total waste of precious time and energy. Many lives have been destroyed by gossip and false rumors spread by malice, jealousy or hate. You can consciously stay out of this vicious ugly circle and discourage it, not so much by arguing a point but by changing the subject, or if you want to be precise, by pointing out that it is nothing but ugly gossip or by simply walking away. No one is obliged or forced to join in gossip. You will also be happier with yourself and in turn project happy energy inviting happy energy back to you. You will find yourself gaining vigor and vitality and good happy valuable people will gravitate to you.

As important as it is that you keep active, it is always wise to keep in mind the law of Balance.

Do not exaggerate and go overboard with excessive activities. Being busy just for the sake of being active, rushing about frantically putting yourself under pressure is not the right idea. Be aware of the quality of your activity and the reason why you have chosen to pursue this particular activity. If you find yourself under tremendous time pressure not having any spare time for the important issues in life, then it is time that you stop to re-evaluate your priorities and to re-arrange your activities. Always keep in mind the balance of trinity, which again is according to how you feel, your own level of energy and personal needs at the moment. If you need only 6 hours of sleep, fine, then you'll have more time for creative work and leisure. If you find that you need 10 hours of sleep regularly, that's fine too. The idea is to be in touch with yourself and your own needs, which can change, to listen to these inner impulses and then to keeping a healthy balance. As we grow and as our lives change, our personal needs and our priorities obviously change too.

## *EXERCISE*

## *to maximize your energy level—*

There is an old universal proverb that says simply 'Practice makes Perfect'. Here is a practical way to put this to work for you.

The longer and the more regularly you practice an activity, the easier it becomes. Pick up an activity, anything, it can be an instrument, an intellectual activity or sport. Begin to practice for a certain period of time if possible every day, or at least three times a week. You practice and at first you will find it difficult, then you will improve a little and you might even begin to enjoy it, and it continues to become easier and easier the more you practice. After a while you improve some more and you reach a stage, where you find the activity pretty comfortable requiring less and less effort on your part. Now you begin to really enjoy it. The stage you have reached here is known as your 'comfort zone.' This means that whatever activity you are practicing has now become routine for you, a habit, and it now requires much less effort and concentration from you than when you started.

At this stage you have three choices to make. You can either stop the activity altogether with the thought that you have achieved what you started out to do and you lose interest, so you go on to something else. Or you can continue on the same level enjoying it, quite content with your accomplishment, but with no desire to achieve more. Or you may decide that with more effort you can perhaps improve even more and become an expert. Let's say you choose the third path and you want to improve even more and do even better. This would now mean, that you would have to exert yourself, to extend the same effort and energy that you did at the very beginning, in order for you to improve and be better than what you are now. You do that, and you repeat the same experience of feeling, of habit and enjoyment, until you find yourself arriving once again at another comfort zone level. Only this time, once again, it is a higher comfort zone level. Keep this up and continue on this level for a period of time. Now you have your three choices again. If you decide you still want to move further, then you push yourself a little more, calling for energy from your reservoir, whether it is your body muscles, brain muscles or emotional muscles, pumping a little more energy into the activity, and you improve your performance once again, moving to a higher level, to yet another comfort zone level. You can repeat this as many times as you like. This is how people become experts at whatever it is they do. It is this constant effort input into the activity of choice. This works on all levels, physical, emotional, mental and spiritual.

Having the desire to improve yourself means that you are able to do it. The extra energy that you need is within you, it is in your own reservoir, and you can draw from this whenever you want to make the effort. You do not need tablets or any other stimuli. All you need is the desire, the will and the effort. Most people are usually too lazy to make that extra step. The effort required is too much. It requires will power, discipline and patience. All that is considered hard work. Musicians, dancers, writers, artists, educators, sportsmen, businessmen and women and all who want to excel in their field of interest use this method. It is not a new discovery. You can actually keep on improving yourself to get better and better, in any activity, as much as you want to. The more effort you invest into the activity, the better you will become, at the same time the stronger you will be as a person. Everyone can do this as long as one is ready to make the effort. The skills that you acquire through hard work are never lost. It is like learning to ride a bicycle or drive a car. It is like learning to swim, to read and write. You never forget it once you have learned it. Once you have built up your muscles, in any area, the result is yours to enjoy. Our ability to improve and excel is infinite.

## *EXERCISE*

## *Meditation to recharge your Energy Reservoir—*

Stretch yourself to get rid of all stiffness and tension in your body. Sit down comfortably on a chair or on the floor. Your hands rest loosely on your thighs or knees palms up. Make sure that your spine is straight. Close your eyes and relax. Breathe in deeply – hold – and breathe out long relaxing your muscles – and hold – breathe in down to your stomach – hold – breathe out and relax, and so forth, seven times. The rhythm can be whatever you feel comfortable with. As you are breathing with a steady rhythm, you are first concentrating on relaxing your whole body. Imagine you are a leaf falling down from a tree, light, falling down, down and down. Then relax to breathing slowly and quietly always pausing in between each breath. Now shift your mind to concentrate on your stomach area. This is where you store your energy and with each breath you take in to your stomach, you imagine breathing in energy from the universe. Imagine yourself having plugged in on to the universal energy power. Do this for fine minutes every day if you can on a regular basis. Or whenever you have a need.

Once you have managed to master the technique, you can recharge your energy reservoir anywhere within a few minutes. I make a habit of doing this exercise during my morning walks in the forest, in the sauna, under the shower, or outside when the sun is shining bright. Sun and water are great sources of energy. The right music can energize you. The company of positive people can energize you. Inspiration can energize you. A good movie can inspire and energize you. Color, water, fresh air, and sun can energize you. You take your choice all it needs is for you to be aware. Be aware of the company you keep and the music you expose yourself to.

*Margo Kirtikar Ph.D*

# V – Be a Possibility Thinker

*Turn problems to challenges,*
*and obstacles to opportunities.*
*Negative experiences are a learning process.*

*'A positive mental attitude is one of the*
*greatest forms of prevention of ill health known*
*to mankind,' says Napoleon Hill. He also says*
*'Mental attitude is also a factor which*
*determines whether one's prayers bring*
*negative or positive results.'*

It takes as much energy to live an unhappy life as a happy one. If you use half of that energy and put it into enjoying your life you will be doing pretty well. Change your No to a Yes. Instead of saying No impossible, to all that comes to you, acquire a possibility thinking attitude, and learn to say: ' Yes, why not?' I personally have lived with this motto all my life and when I arrived in New York and realized that everyone thought and lived the same way, I fell in love with New York and spent fourteen years of my life there.

Change in life, good or bad, is a part of life's learning process and the degree of learning and development depends on the response of each individual to the personal experiences.

Development depends on the willingness and the ability of the person to experience life positively. Self trust is the secret of a positive mental attitude. Goethe went further to say ' *As soon as you can trust yourself you will know how to live.'* Those who welcome life with open arms and minds, have the ability to meet adversity and failure, sorrow and misfortune, with calmness and a smile. They do not lose their enthusiasm but keep on going forward, if anything, with a higher level of energy. Instead of panicking they probe for answers and solutions. A temporary failure to them is nothing but an incident from which they draw know-how and experience and added strength. Each time you encounter a set back and you overcome it, you emerge from it stronger than before.

A person with an open heart and mind is a positive attitude person with a 'possibility thinking' program. Mental attitude is contagious. A positive person's energy acts like a magnet and draws others with similar energy towards it. It is the habit of a positive person to look for the good qualities in other people, and at the same time is prepared to accept and have compassion for any unfavorable qualities found. There is a joyful exchange of life experiences, and a harmonious flowing of life. A positive person is like a happy house with wide open doors and windows, allowing the sunshine in, full of light and fresh air. Inside it is warm, clean and inviting, making everyone feel welcome and comfortable. When meeting a problem, a positive person responds with many creative possibilities as possible solutions to the problem. Imagine mental attitude as having two doors, and you have the choice to use either door, the one door is labeled negative and the other positive. You have the freedom to choose which mental attitude you want to live with.

The person who is in the habit of saying 'No, impossible...' is not aware of nature's laws and usually ends up watching the person who is doing it. The one who has chosen to act has not only recognized the changing circumstances but has adapted to them and is always one step ahead. A negative person establishes his own limitations in his own mind, allowing himself to be influenced by negative outside forces. This person usually sees the worse side in everything and finds it difficult to find solutions when problems arise, because he is too busy accumulating feelings of hate, resentments, revenge, and envy, blocking his mind. His mind becomes cluttered with these negative thoughts and criticisms and his discontent in time effects his attitude. A negative person is like a house, uncared for with all the shutters down to keep the sunlight away. Inside it is dark and dismal, piled with old heavy furniture, dusty and full of cobwebs. The house never gets fresh air and no one wants to get near it.

Failure or misfortune hits everyone of us at some time or another. Our attitude towards such misfortunes and our ability to deal with them determines the course of our life. A negative person would find each problem a total catastrophe unable to deal with the situation and incapable of finding workable solutions. For a positive person on the other hand, every problem has a solution. Imagine having a problem on the one side and the solution on the other side, and you have a choice which side you want to concentrate on. The more concentration you put to finding the solution, the more chance you have to solve the problem. The more you concentrate on the problem itself, however, the less chance you will have to find a solution.

Negative thinkers will often insist on looking at reality. 'Be realistic' they love to say. But they do not have any solutions. Whereas positive thinkers will say, ' Well, look at this way. You could this or you could do that...,' giving you something to think about. The negative thinkers might again insist, ' No, that's not good because of….' focusing on the problem and telling you again that you are not being realistic. More likely than not they would rub it in and give you the famous 'I told you so' routine. The positive thinkers, if unable to help you with an immediate solution, will at least have compassion with you and try to encourage you not to give up.

Remember, your reality is what you see for yourself. My reality can be different from your reality, because I am looking at a situation from my point of view, depending on my life experiences and the conditioning of my thoughts and my feelings. I see the problem with my eyes and with my mind. The very same problem can look totally different from your point of view, since you have different life experiences to mine. If we are both positive people, that is great, because between us, we will have at least two solutions and most probably even more. Imagine what it would be like if we were both negative. We would be sitting there, stuck with this problem which becomes double size, and we would be realistically looking at our reality and we would both be miserable, focusing on the limitations and finding no solution at all.

I would like to tell you about someone I know whom I will name Frank. Frank is a young man in his early thirties and has been out of a job for over a year. All his attempts at finding a new job have so far been unsuccessful. He is a typical victim of economic circumstances.

Frank, unfortunately, is a negative thinker. He tends to see the worst side in everything. His mind is totally closed to self-growth or any kind of self-help. He does not exactly exude energy and spends much of his time in bars drinking, smoking and talking to others who have similar problems and who are likewise negative about life in general. He and the friends with whom he hangs around, are convinced that there is nothing they can do to change their situation. They see themselves as victims of their circumstances and feel helpless. They are full of self-pity for themselves and each other.

Here are some – Positive Thinking Possibilities – of what Frank could be doing for himself.

First he could sit down with paper and pencil and begin to count his blessings. We all have blessings, in one way or another, no matter how rough the times are, or how badly off we are.

He could write for example:

I am healthy

I am young

I am intelligent

I am educated
I have the basic necessities of life
I have a family who loves me
I have friends who care about me
I have contacts I could make good use of
I have no other responsibility but to myself
I am mobile and free to travel

That is a total of ten blessings and should make him feel pretty good about himself.

Next Frank should write down his problem in detail for example:

No job/no regular income (circumstances beyond his control)

Drink/alcohol (his own doing)

Inertia – no energy (his own doing)

Negativity/worry/self pity/fear (his own doing)

Those are four points. When we look at the blessings versus problems on paper, the whole situation takes on another dimension. We can see clearly that Frank's blessings are much greater compared to his problems. We also see that three of the listed problems are self-inflicted and could be eliminated immediately if Frank decided to take action and discipline himself. The choice is his to make. Frank is making life miserable for Frank! Not only that, but Frank is probably also making his family and everyone close to him miserable too.

A plan for action for Frank would be:

- to stop his drinking immediately, perhaps also smoking.

- to begin on a program to gain his self confidence and self worth.

- to use discipline in his life style, start exercise, sports, jogging etc.

- to continue educating himself professionally if possible.

- to go out and look for any odd job, even volunteer work if there's nothing else available. At this point for him any work is better than no work.

Obviously he will need help and support to put him back on the right track. He could make an effort either to find a self-help group he can join or visit some workshops regularly. The odd jobs will help him to keep active and at the same time in circulation and in contact with people. Even if he does not make money at the start, helping others will make him feel happier about himself. He will gain self-respect. His family will be happier too for him. He will have more energy and vitality so he still pursues regularly looking out for a regular job. He can talk to everyone he meets and keep his ears open. If and when he goes back to the bar for a drink he will have something to talk about and will attract others who are also active like himself. After some time by the law of Averages, he is bound to find new doors and new opportunities leading him to a new job and a new existence.

To summarize:

Itemize your blessings and write them down, including your hobbies. Sometimes one can turn one's hobby into a money making project

Itemize your problems and write them down. Be honest and list them all. Seeing problems on paper reduces the terror and will make them more manageable.

List all your solution possibilities. Let your imagination loose, whatever you can think of even if the ideas seem illogical and far-fetched.

Act now without further delay. Remember nothing works by itself. It is up to you to take action and to make things happen. You must move the energy around you the way you want it to go by moving first.

Keep in mind that, as a rule, help comes only to those who help themselves.

Keep your mind focused on your goal. Make sure to have short, immediate, easy, achievable goals. Be flexible to go with the flow, however, and do not hesitate to change your course of action if necessary, if you have to, as long as you feel that it is right for you. Who knows perhaps it will lead you indirectly to your original goal. One way to recognize whether you are going with the flow or not is by observing results of your attempts, as you aspire after something. If you keep getting closed doors or you face problems with every step you take, take this as a sign that you are possibly doing something wrong and you are going against the flow. Relax, take a step back, and reevaluate your goal and your intentions. You will know and feel when you are going with the flow of things completely. When every step you take is achieved with great ease, without too much effort or stress on your part. When you find doors opening for you the moment you knock, and help is given to you when you need it, then this definitely is a sign that you are going with the flow and that it is right for you.

According to the law of Attraction positive people attract positive experiences and negative people attract negative experiences. When you maintain a positive mind, you are going to find that negative thinking people will automatically start avoiding you the same as you yourself avoid them. More and more you will gravitate to positive people and people with a positive outlook on life will gravitate to you.

Buddha said:

> *A man believes a thing when he behaves*
> *as if it were true.*
> *You believe you are a winner, you*
> *become a winner,*
> *you believe that you are a loser and you*
> *are a loser.*

It is quite normal and even necessary to have both the negative and the positive energies in order to function and have the right orientation in practical life. The natural negative part is as useful and practical as the positive part of us. For example when we sense displeasure or danger nearing a fire, etc. our instinct immediately warns us with a NO stopping us from burning ourselves and getting hurt. Only the greater part of our negative emotions are self fabricated and self damaging and we can easily become addicted to these negative feelings. Some peoples' lives are regulated, controlled and ultimately ruined by mechanical negative thoughts and emotions. In reality, negativity is nothing but weakness and often even the beginning of depression, insanity, hysteria or crime. No inner development or unity is possible as long as one is addicted to negativity. It is possible to conquer this addiction to negative emotional fixations when we understand the danger involved.

## *EXERCISES*

## *to develop a positive mental attitude—*

1. Before dropping off to sleep, go over your experiences of the day, forgive anyone who annoyed you or hurt you in any way, and if you have hurt anyone else, ask the universe for forgiveness. Make sure that you mean it otherwise you would be cheating yourself and it will have no positive effect. Forgiveness is a very important character trait that cleanses negativity. Your heart will fill with love when you have learned to forgive. Love is healing. Pure unconditional love is what life is all about. Love for yourself, for mankind and for the whole universe.

2. Upon waking up and before you get out of bed each morning, be grateful that you can live another day. You are a miracle and you should not be taking your life for granted. Remember your life can be taken away from you

without warning any second. Learn to be aware of your life and to live it well. Being grateful for your life, for who you are, for the things you have and whatever you can be.

3.   Make a copy of the negative and positive attributes list that you find at the end of this book and hang it up somewhere where you can see it every day. Try your best to eliminate the negative feelings from your mind and to acquire the positive feelings. This will need awareness and patience but if you make an effort, after a while you will notice the difference in your life. A positive person must be so from deep within the psyche and not only superficially. In other words, if you speak positive words but buried deep down inside you are doubts, fears, hate, resentments and other negativity, then you are not genuinely positive. You would have to face your true inner self and be very honest, acknowledge and accept your negative feelings. Try to control and to discard them slowly and diligently one by one and to replace

them with positive traits by practicing this daily throughout your life and true inner peace will be your reward.

# VI – Free Yourself of Your Chains

*The world mirrors what is inside you.*

I remember my grandmother in Damascus, when I must have been no more than ten years old, explaining to me, how everyone of us is born with an invisible cross that we have to carry around with us as long for as we live. Everyone without exception carries this invisible cross which varies in size and weight according to the way they live their life. *'Never envy anyone for who they are and what they have.'* She continued, *'never wish to be someone else, because you have no idea how heavy the cross is that they are carrying. If you wish you were in their place and your wish comes true, you might end up carrying their cross which might be a lot heavier than your is. Be happy with yourself and your cross, whatever it is.'* I adored my grandmother and I feared her because she was very strict, both at the same time and her words of wisdom had a tremendous impact on me. I have a very vivid imagination because I was cured instantaneously for life of all hate, envy, jealousy and greed. I did not want to carry any unnecessary extra burdens!

What made all what I heard more dramatic, was that it was good Friday and being raised in the Christian faith, images of Jesus carrying the cross were everywhere, making the picture very vivid for me. My imagination went wild. I went around after that seeing this phantom cross on everyone's shoulders and I could actually feel the size and weight of the cross each person was carrying. It was easy for me to see, the look in the individual's eyes, the way the person talked, moved and carried her or himself, the behavior and words were all a give away of this intimate secret. I still see this today except that I have replaced the cross symbol with a huge invisible bag.

It is true no one is spared hardships and misfortunes in life. It is also true and good to remember not to feel, hate, anger, greed, envy and jealousy for others but to be content with whom we are, and to be thankful that our burden is not bigger than it is. My grandmother, over fifty years ago had no choice. Being in Damascus, and a woman, she had to resign to the circumstances of her life and bear it. She decided to accept this fact and to carry her cross with dignity. And this is still true, believable or not, today in many parts of the world where women are still shamelessly suppressed and treated as slaves. We, who are more lucky in the western world, know differently. We know that it is up to each one of us to take responsibility for our own individual lives, and that we have the freedom to do this. We know that we are responsible for our own happiness independent of others. We know that our thoughts, attitude and awareness determine our state of happiness and that true freedom comes from within, the same as beauty and strength.

Now imagine yourself with a huge expandable bag, tied to your shoulders with chains, as an intimate invisible part of you. This bag has many compartments with the labels, hate, fear, inertia, bad habits, resentments and miscellaneous negative. Since your childhood and it begins from the day you were conceived, you are either filling this bag yourself, or else other people in your life dump garbage into your various compartments. You, not having the awareness nor the know how to deal with it, carry this bag around with you trying not to show it. Only when someone comes by and dumps a particularly heavy load into your bag, you lose control, get angry and confused, you break down or you cry your heart out. You might try to find satisfaction, refuge and comfort by getting addicted to a person, drug, drink, work, hobby or food. You might find an outlet by criticizing or tyrannizing those close to you or much worse still you might turn into a criminal. The list is endless.

The fact is that it is totally unnecessary for you to carry this heavy burden and have it get heavier and heavier as you get older. It is not only your right to free yourself but you have the ability and the power in your own hands to do so. You can empty your load and free yourself of your chains, all you need to do is to have the wish to dump your load, The world mirrors back to you what is inside you. Your bag load might be invisible to the physical eye but in reality whatever it is your bag expresses itself through your behavior. The negative quality of the load you have in your bag determines your thought patterns and your actions. If your words do not give you away, your attitude certainly will, You might not be conscious of this but people around you feel your vibrations.

## *Free Yourself of Negativity*

Hari Prasad Shastri (Direct Experience of Reality) says,

*'...all being the one Self whom shall we hate, whom shall we consider a stranger?'*

The law of Substitution says, you can only think one thought at a time. Choose to control your thoughts and make each of your thoughts, pleasant, constructive and positive. Chronic negativity not only weighs you down heavily, limits you in every way but it can also be a burden on others who have to deal with you. You might have a tendency to harbor negative thoughts deep down inside you, which you never articulate. Your true innermost feelings and thoughts, however, do have an impact on your behavior. Negativity shows in your body posture, in the tone of your voice and in your attitude. To be free of your negative nature you need to shift your awareness to concentrate on building up your positive nature.

Your brain is constantly at work and is like a chatterbox, even when you are asleep, producing unintelligent chatter both negative and positive depending upon your inclination to one or the other. Depending on how you perceive your world your thoughts might exist of endless negative useless and damaging chatter, that has nothing to do with reality at all. There are many reasons why you might be harboring negative feelings and thoughts. It could be insecurity, hurt from the past, guilt, envy, fear or resentments. Analyze yourself to find out for yourself what it could be, look at it and acknowledge it, understand, forgive and throw away the useless and unpleasant. What is past is gone and if you imagine the bag you are carrying on your shoulders, it should be easier for you to understand why you have to begin to lighten your load, so that you can be free to live a constructive life. It is in your power to call on the inner Self, to take control of your thought, to make sure that they are warm, positive and constructive. Whatever you focus your attention to, your thought dwell on, and the longer you spend on negative thoughts, the less you have time to discover your true self and your true talents.

Gossip is a negative activity and is one of the worst self destructive past time and a major obstacle to discovering the inner Self. Far too many people indulge in gossip without realizing the damage they are causing by spreading negative energy around. One usually gossips about someone, spreading false harmful rumors, because one feels inadequate, jealous, resentful, or envious of the person. No one encourages nor joins in gossip, unless one shares these self-destructive negative traits. Be aware and observe your self, next time you are tempted or caught in gossip and question yourself of your true motives. Remember you are exposing no one but your own insecurities while you gossip about someone else. Do your best to stop and to stay far away from people who thrive on gossip and criticism of others.

If you hate someone and you have to deal with them anyway for reasons beyond your control then accept the situation for what it is and make an effort to have a friendly relationship. Remember that we are all divine beings, interdependent and interconnected with each other. If you keep this in mind it might make it easier for you to deal with people you dislike or with people who have hurt you. Try not to judge nor criticize others, remember that you also have faults, find instead and concentrate on their good points, everyone has some. Remember there are only two kinds of thoughts for you to choose from, pleasant thoughts that make you feel good and unpleasant thoughts that make you feel bad. Why would you choose to make yourself feel bad? Other than that the feelings of resentment, hate and that of revenge, for whatever reason, are pure poison and do more harm to the person who hates than to the hated.

*Margo Kirtikar Ph.D*

## *Free Yourself of Fear*

*Facing the unknown, we are paralyzed with fear.*
'He who knows himself has conquered fear.'
*According to Sri Shankaracharya, great Indian Philosopher (788-820 AD.)*

Seven basic fears many of us suffer from are criticism, ill health, loss of love, old age, death, fear of our own emotions and misfortune and these fears create in us indifference, indecision, doubt, worry, laziness, overreaction, stubbornness and procrastination. Fear, anxiety and worry paralyze our emotions, limit our freedom and block our ability to think clearly and constructively. *'Fear is our greatest enemy. It cripples our judgement and robs us of all initiative to do good and to make investigations into truth. Fear is poison. When we come to know the Self we lose our fear.'* (The Upanishad, Penguin, 1981.)

You fear criticism when you have a low self-esteem and feel you are inferior to others. People with self-confidence do not fear criticism. No one can give you self worth, only you can give yourself self worth. it is up to you to build up your self-image. Concentrate to begin with on your physical body, the healthier you are the better you feel about yourself and the more attractive you will be. Keeping a healthy diet, exercising, keeping your weight under control, will inspire you to dress well. As a result you will suffer less ill health and you will carry yourself with more confidence. Be aware of what company you keep and make sure that you surround yourself with warm loving people, who are supportive and if anything might give you helpful constructive criticism. With both a positive attitude and a higher self-esteem you will find that you will enjoy better health.

Nature dictates your aging process and leaves you no choice. It is a natural process that we all have to accept. Rather than fight it work with it. You cannot control your age but you can learn to enjoy your age, whatever it is, and look forward to enjoying every stage for your life, as you grow older. There is a special charm to every age group. The better you feel about yourself the more attractive and youthful you will be. Age brings peace, wisdom and grace along with it, which should be appreciated and not feared. In living a life full of love and harmony, contributing to life in your world in your own way, there is no need to fear death. You will have a clear conscience and be at peace with yourself, if you have chronic fears that you find difficult to get rid of, it is a good idea to talk to someone about it, a friend, a relative, a therapist, a doctor or a priest. Talk to anyone whom you can trust and feel comfortable with. Talking about your fear openly to someone who will listen to you and have compassion with you can in itself be a very freeing experience.

Weaknesses, fears, hates, guilt and resentments can grow inside you if you allow them to become ugly monsters that eat away at you from the inside. One of the most painful experiences is when you are actually facing one of these inner monsters. All of us have these inner monsters in different shapes and sizes, some more and some less. Unless you acknowledge this and get them out into the open one by one, face them, analyze them, understand them and then consciously throw them out of your system, you will be stuck with them for the rest of your life. It is you who hang on to these ugly inner pains and hurts and not the other way round. Negative feelings and experiences, when accumulated and kept inside you undigested over a long period of time, do not only make you physically unattractive, but can also be dangerous to your health. I often think of the stories and the many movies I saw as a child of Sindbad the Sailor. Sindbad who through his many journeys, met again and again with big ugly terrifying beasts, and he could not go on with his journey unless he either killed or outsmarted the monster blocking his progress. Somehow, I see Sindbad's monsters in the fairy tale, representing all the negative and painful feelings inside me from all my life experiences, which I am supposed to overcome in order for me to move on free without a heavy baggage, on my own journey through life and self realization. In the same way someone explained to me once the actual meaning of the image of St. George sitting on the horse and holding the dragon down with a spear. St. George represents the Divine in the human being holding the dragon, inner negativity or lower self, constantly under control or else the dragon or inner negativity, will conquer the divine in the human being.

We actually fear the unknown, so the more we keep ourselves informed the less we need to fear. A simple example, parents worry where their daughter is and why she is late coming home. If the parents know where the daughter is and if the daughter calls home when delayed, there would be no need for the parents to worry. Worry is a negative energy and is harmful to the person who is worrying as well as to the object of worry. By concentrating one's energy on a thought long enough one can make it manifest. If you are driving a car and you worry about having an accident, the worry will make you so tense that you will most likely end up with an accident to which you would probably think 'I knew it!' Another example is a student who fears exams and is so sick with worry that he or she will fail the exam. Worrying makes the student tense and tension blocks the energy flow, which in turn, blocks clear thinking resulting with the mind going blank or reading the question incorrectly. Instead of worrying, the student could make better use of the energy and time by studying the subject thoroughly beforehand, be well prepared and arrive promptly on the exam day fresh and relaxed to assure best performance.

The same principle goes for a professional who is nervous and fearful of the outcome of an important presentation or meeting. If you focus your energy on being physically, emotionally and mentally well prepared you are confident of your performance that will guarantee you success. If you focus your energy on worry or fear of what the result might or might not be, your emotions are blocked, your thoughts are scattered and you are physically so tense that it is impossible for you to give your best.

You can only rid yourself of your fears if your are willing to acknowledge and face them for what they are. Analyze rationally what you are really afraid of and what would be the worst thing to happen if your fear does come true. Once this is clear you can then work out the alternatives of what actions you can take to protect yourself. Two good thoughts to always keep in mind. One is that nothing is as bad as it may seem and two, there is always a solution to every problem. We are usually afraid of the unknown and looking it straight in the eye, i.e. face the monster, it helps us to get over our fear. Keep reminding yourself taking action is better use of your energy and emotions than being afraid. When you have learned to overcome some of your fears, you will begin to experience a new sensation of freedom, feeling both strength and light at the same time, discovering a strength that comes from deep within you giving you self confidence and a mobility of thoughts and movement. You will be able to handle adverse circumstances and unwelcome situations without breaking down under the pressure.

Another feeling that is connected with fear is worry. Many people live in constant worry and anguish about one thing or another not realizing that worrying about something or someone is selfish and absolutely useless. Instead of blocking your thoughts with worries, free your mind so that you can have genuine constructive helpful thoughts in order to be of help. 'I worry about you' is a sentence many use without really being of any help. Worry is a negative feeling. It is fine and understandable to be concerned about someone, if you have a good reason to be concerned, but then accompany this feeling of concern with a helpful definite positive action, in whatever way possible. For example, a simple sentence such as 'I am concerned about you. I am here, if you need any help.' Or ' I care about you well being, if I can help you in any way, tell me. Or ' I feel with you. I will include you in my prayers.' Of course you have to mean what you say. This is a thousand times more helpful than just telling someone you worry about them.

## *Free Yourself of Bad Habits*

*First we form our habits*
*And then our habits form us.*

It is habit that makes it difficult for you to deal with change in your life. You might be set so deep in your habits that your whole body, intellect, feelings and physical, fight the new situation and unless you reprogram your habits to adapt to the new circumstances, you will continue to be miserable. The less changes you have in your life the more you become a slave to your habits, the deeper you are set in your habits and the less you can cope with change. The less receptive you are to new input, the less creative you are, and the more unhappy you will be when a change is imposed on you, upsetting your habitual ways of operating, thinking and living.

One way to be quick in adapting to change is to make a habit of consciously and continuously changing your habits. This keeps you in practice and subsequently finding it easier to adapt and re-adapt whenever you have to. For you to control your habits rather than be slave to them, you must first be aware of these habits. Then make a point of changing your habits often. The more often you are able to change your small habits, the easier it will be come. Chew gum instead of smoking for a whole day, drink water or juice instead of alcohol for a week, read a magazine or listen to the radio instead of watching TV now and again. Walk up some stairs instead of taking the elevator sometimes, whatever it is, decide consciously to do it differently. What you gain with this is the continuous exercise of readapting, without great effort needed. Any change of habit is difficult for the first few days, with time though it does get easier. When you have accustomed yourself to changing your habits often, you will be better equipped to deal with the changes in your life that are imposed upon you and you will not fall apart that easily at the challenges put in your way.

Observe yourself and your habits and question yourself why you do one thing one way and the other another way. Ask yourself, are these thoughts you are now thinking really your own or are they the thoughts of others which you have acquired, your parents perhaps, or your teachers, friends or partner? Reshuffle your thoughts and see if you cannot come up with your own ideas and thoughts. Acquire the good habit of being in control of your own thoughts rather than accepting the thoughts of others as your own. Some habits you are aware of, others, however, are so much integrated in you that they seem like second nature to you and you do not even recognize them as habits. Learn to differentiate the good from the bad habits, which should be easy, good habits are a pain and sometimes require extra effort but they make you feel good and bad habits are fun but make you feel guilty and are usually self destructive. As an example of a good habit is an early morning walk which would mean waking up early every day, no matter what time you go to bed. Or having a cold shower every morning or reading a book before going to sleep. You might not always feel like doing one or the other but when you do you feel a lot better. A bad habit is being chronically late for all your appointment for example or losing your temper for any minor thing that might go wrong.

It is not possible to get rid of a bad habit by willing it away intellectually. The wish to change has to happen from much deeper with in you. It is within your power to change your habits if you really long for this change passionately. This deep desire with all your feelings, with all your being is a prerequisite. Once you have this, you require discipline and determination to go through with the desired change. When the desire is genuine, the discipline and the determination will be effortless. If you have to force yourself then your heart is not in it. The Law of Nature does not allow a vacuum, even as you empty a glass of water it refills with air. This means, simply, that you cannot break an old habit unless you replace it with a new habit. Which habits you want to hang on to is your choice, more important is being aware that you have your habits. If you are in the habit of gossiping, develop an interest in

209

general knowledge and talk about your acquired knowledge instead and avoid people who gossip.

Getting rid of old habits will bring you to a new awareness of yourself, it will give you a new experience and will bring you new thoughts and opportunities. Instead of doing one thing, do something else, instead of doing it one way, try doing it another way. Form an image in your mind of the type of person you would like to be, visualize this constantly and before long you will automatically begin to behave in that way. Your habits and outlook on life play a major part in your happiness and this is something that only you can change. Many unpleasant situations can be improved simply by changing your habitual way of thinking. This is true even though the situation itself remains the same.

## *Face Your Fear*

Take one fear or worry at a time. Write it down on a piece of paper and look at it. Then ask yourself the following questions:

Does this fear make sense?

Is this fear logical. i.e. is it a valid fear?

Does it really help anyone when I feel this fear?

Would anyone suffer if I did not feel this fear any more?

If you answer NO to all questions, then you know that you could throw this fear out of your bag.

If you answer YES to any one question, then you have to analyze why and does that answer make sense, repeating the same process.

Affirmations
Truth rules my life
I am free of fear and worry
I have courage to handle any situation
I am guided and protected by my Higher Self
I have faith that all is well

## Free yourself of Doubts

When you find yourself in a state of panic, when you find your mind crowded with unpleasant thoughts and worries, doubts and uncertainties, make a habit to do the following:

Sit still and realize that your doubts have nothing to do with reality. Your doubts are thoughts caused by your imagination running wild because of fear and therefore playing havoc in your mind. You can stop this by seeking quietness and keeping your wild imagination under control.

Relax your physical body and steady your mind, close your eyes so that you can focus your attention. Now in your mind's eye visualize yourself surrounded by a pyramid and you are standing in the middle of this pyramid. Imagine this pyramid is connected with the Universe at the top of the pyramid. Now call with a deliberation and force a stream of pure white light and love and see in your imagination, this light and love going through and bathing your form. See your physical body, your emotional and your mental body, being filled with pure white light and being cleansed from all your fears, worries and uncertainties. Feel the light and love going through every cell in your body giving you a sense of peace and calmness. Remember to breathe deep, soft and regular as you concentrate on this picture. If you can make your call aloud, do it, if you cannot then do it silently mentally.

What is important is that you concentrate fully, that you actually see with your inner vision and feel the pyramid, light and love. You can repeat this exercise as many times as you wish until you have made it an established fact of your life. Repeat it periodically whenever you need to reinforce it. This exercise is good to do when you feel tired. Try it out and have patience. It really works.

## *Meditation to free yourself of Doubts and Fears —*

*This meditation should take you about 15-30 minutes.*

Stretch and relax your body. Sit down in a quiet neat room, on a chair or on the floor with crossed legs yoga style, with your back straight, you can also lie down flat on your back with your arms relaxed by your side, whichever is more comfortable for you. Close your eyes, relax and concentrate on your breathing. Breathe in and out deeply in a steady rhythm, naturally without forcing anything. Always pause a while in between each breath, remembering breathing out is as important as breathing in, concentrate on your breathing and repeat slowly twelve times. Feel your body relaxing, slow down your breathing and feel yourself relaxing some more. Keep on breathing slowly and relaxing.

Now imagine yourself in your mind's eye sitting under a tree by a lake side, it is beautiful and sunny and you are relaxed and happy. You are happy because you have finally made an important decision, which is to get rid of one of your fears. A fear that you have been carrying around with you for some time now. It has been heavy to carry around and weighing you down and you do not want it any more. Build yourself a small fire and sit down comfortably by the fire. Very slowly you imagine yourself picking up this fear, written on a piece of paper and you see yourself slowly throwing this piece of paper with your fear into the fire. As you watch this fear burn into ashes and disappear, you feel great relief and peace.

Relax and contemplate over what you have just done. You have just lightened your load by throwing away one fear that has made you miserable for so long. It is now gone forever. Mourn for all the time that you have suffered in the past. Leave it behind you now and forget it. Watch the fire die down and your fear disappearing into ashes. After a while imagine yourself getting up very slowly and you walking away from the lake enjoying the breeze and the sun feeling free and lighter than ever before.

Gradually you come back to your senses, to the present, you come back bringing with you the lightness, feeling happy and refreshed. You open your eyes, feeling good about yourself, full of energy and vitality, you stretch yourself and you get up slowly.

You can meditate and get rid of all your fear one by one in the same way. If you have a fear that persists meditate on it as many times as necessary, imagine it being too heavy for you to carry so you break it up into parts and imagine yourself burning away one part after another. If it does not work to begin with keep on repeating, perhaps your visualization ability lacks the detail and the passion, so keep on practicing until you see a result. Practice makes perfect.

## Practice changing your Habits—

If you observe your daily routine you will find yourself automatically doing many things out of habit. Try to become aware of this and every day make a point of doing one task different to your usual way. For example if you take one way to go to work, choose another way to change the routine. If you usually read the paper at a certain time every day, do something else instead. Instead of drinking your usual cup of coffee have a cup of tea instead or have a glass of juice. For a change actually see, take into awareness and speak to the salesgirl, receptionist or bus driver whom you see every day but never take any notice of. The idea is that as soon as you notice that you are automatically and absentmindedly doing something out of habit, change the habit so that you are aware of what you are doing forcing yourself to stay awake. Habit puts you to sleep and before you know it you have become a slave to the habit. The famous Sufi Philosopher Gurdjeff described the mass as going through life asleep, i.e. unaware. Gurdjeff's life work was dedicate to awaken people out of their slumber like living.

Good habits are fine as long as they make you feel good. Nevertheless, you should not become a slave to them because when change does come into your life, it will be very painful to give them up. The above exercise is one good solution to be well prepared.

Bad habits usually give us short-term satisfaction but long term they can be very damaging. Write down the bad habits that you want to get rid of and replace with good habits. You might have to force yourself at first but after a few days it will become easier, force yourself to keep on, until you see results. Example; I want to lose weight. I want to lose two kilos. I begin by outlining a detailed plan of how I want to achieve this. I decide that the easiest and the most effective way is for me to cut out my heavy lunches for the period of one week. I choose a short, practical and possible goal for me to achieve. I will reevaluate after one week and then decide if I want to go on to lose more weight. I decide to do the following during my lunch hour. I will eat fruits or raw vegetables with a glass of water first and then go for a half hour brisk walk. When I am back I will have one cup of black coffee.

Everyday in my mind's eye, before going to sleep I decide what I want to eat for lunch tomorrow in detail, which fruit and which vegetable and exactly how many pieces. For instance, I decide to have one orange and one banana. The next day I make sure that I do exactly that. At the end of the week I check my weight and decide if I want to lose more weight to repeat the same for another week.

When I am very precise about my decision and my plan to carry it out, I am disciplining myself and concentrating on a program. This way I know exactly what I have to do when lunchtime comes and I will not be tempted or talked into doing something else. It is easier for me to stick to this rigid program for one week assuring me success.

I am making sure that I am replacing my old habit of eating a big meal at my favorite restaurant every lunchtime, with a healthier plan of eating fruits and vegis and a short walk. I am definite and disciplined about what I want to do and how I want to do it. This is a good practice for contact with the inner Self. Choose something, make a plan that is reasonable and stick to it. This is also an excellent exercise for self discipline.

## VII – Now is your Future

Confucius said:
*'It is better to turn the light on than to complain about the darkness.'*

Life is a miracle. I see life as a gift and each day is a new beginning. I see a chance to start each day fresh again and again from scratch. Each day brings a new fresh beginning for every one of us and even if you try something and you fail, there is no reason why you should not try again and again, every single day. Do not allow your consciousness to be dominated by demands and expectations based on the dead past or the imagined future. Today, here and now is the reality in your life and it is only from the conditions of the present that your future can be generated. Any moment, any time, is the right moment for you to stop complaining about the dark. You can turn on the light in your life.

When you tune in to the present moment in your life, you will find that you have the ability to enjoy every moment without limitations. If you dominate your conscious with thoughts of the past or the future, you can hardly enjoy the moment. Any thoughts dealing with wishes to own something you do not have, living in or dwelling on the past, or dreaming about the future are keeping you away from living the moment. Trying to hold on to old things which are no longer appropriate in the present flow of your life, blocks you from living the moment and from moving forward. Tuning in to the moment now opens a whole new horizon for you.

Most people keep themselves in misery, on a lower consciousness level, by endlessly chatting about what they did in the past or what happened to them in the past. Old hurts or old loves. Past achievements or long passed misfortunes. Other people forget the past and focus on dreaming about a future. Your past is important to you because it is your foundation that you cannot and should not deny. You cannot deny where you were born, who your parents were and you cannot deny your roots. You can also not deny your achievements nor your misfortunes. You carry all those experiences with you of course, however, it is not who you are today at this moment. It is good to accept the past, both the good and the bad. Do not pretend that an unhappy past did not exist and do not create false images of the past either. Nothing survives time that is not built on truth.

At the same time it is good to have goals in life, without a definite goal you do not arrive anywhere. But sitting back and dreaming about a far away future, doing nothing towards it, or being active with a definite goal in mind towards a future, are two different things. Dreaming is passive with you sitting in the audience seat uninvolved watching a dream, similar to you watching a movie scene with other people acting. Having and visualizing a goal, however, is active with you involved as director, producer and actor playing an important role to make the scene manifest. In simple terms, no dream will come true unless you make a personal commitment and effort to make it happen which brings us back to the awareness of living the present moment 'now.'

The concept of living in the present moment, unfortunately, is often misunderstood. Some interpret it to mean that one should enjoy oneself totally, indulge in whatever makes one happy, regardless whether it is harmful or not, forgetting tomorrow and having no consideration for others. This is a gross misinterpretation. Living in the present moment means understanding that your past has brought you to where you are now, but now, will also shape your tomorrow and will effect your future. When you live every present moment consciously, being aware of your thoughts, your actions and your behavior then you will be accumulating many moments and days, weeks, months and years of good constructive behavior. Every now which becomes yesterday will consist of quality memories and your tomorrow will always be better and better. Every moment lived with awareness makes up a good day, like a good solid brick and you pile up all your good days like good solid bricks, forming your future.

About twenty years ago, I was in an accident which almost cost me my life. Until then I was under the impression that I had always lived my life intensively with total awareness. I was wrong. Lying helpless in bed, I realized how I had taken so many things for granted in my life. After the accident I acquired a totally different perception to life and my relationships to everyone around me changed completely. And most specifically with my loved ones. It was as if I had on a different pair of glasses through which I perceived the world and could see much more clearly than before. I became much more aware of my feelings and my behavior to others. In the same way, I thought I was always aware of time, but I was wrong again. I learned to have more respect for time and became much more conscious of how I made use of my time.

A good exercise to gain awareness of the present is to imagine to yourself that this is the first meeting you are having with whomever you are with, and you are never going to see them again. Imagine this is the last day you are spending with your family. You will be surprised at the change in your attitude and at the way you see and deal with them soaking in every detail with intensity. Whenever you are discontent and unhappy, imagine yourself in a worse situation than the one you are in presently. Imagine what it would be like if you were blind. Tie a scarf around your eyes for half an hour and try to walk around and to do something. Feel what it is like to be blind. This is a good exercise not to take your eyesight for granted and you will begin to actually see with awareness. Imagine you have lost an arm, tie one arm behind you and try to live half a day or even a few hours like this. Observe your feelings, your thoughts and what you experience as you try out this exercise.

One habit I adopted at a very young age, before I was ten, happened unintentionally. I was very unhappy and dissatisfied with my life and everything in general, including my parents and school. I remember feeling very sorry for myself.

Bored to tears, I sat in my room and picked up a book to read. The story was about a young girl somewhere in Africa who had been kidnapped and sold into slavery. I probably did not understand most of what I was reading but what I did understand was the misery that this girl was going through and I cried for her. I cried for her and I forgot about myself. Then it occurred to me how lucky I was that I had a home and parents who took care that no harm came to me. I felt warm, protected and loved. My self-pity, anger and resentment melted away to be replaced by gratitude and love for my parents. I was thankful that fate was kinder to me. Ever since that experience, I have made it my habit, whenever I feel unhappy about my life or circumstances, to remember or to read about other people's misery and hardships. Or I imagine how much worse things could be for me, which immediately makes me feel better, putting me back on the right track again. I do this consciously and it works every time without fail. It frees me to live and to appreciate the moment whatever it is and to be grateful for having what I have.

It is an exercise that you can try out for yourself. It will need some discipline at first and you might find yourself slipping back into your old habits again and again, but with understanding, persistence and practice you will be able to live and to enjoy the present moment more often than not. The goal you want to achieve is to live with more awareness and to be grateful for who you are and what you are. To be grateful for your life and what you have. Being grateful is a good daily exercise to heighten your awareness.

## EXERCISE

## *to practice being in the Moment—*

Have a meeting with your wife, husband, child or friend. Pretend this is the last time you will ever see or meet them again. Watch how aware you are, of every little detail of the meeting, trying to imprint in your memory, the way they look concentrating on every word they say. Observe yourself and your choice of words, your own attitude and behavior. You will be experiencing an intensive living in the now.

Pretend you have no past and no future, forget who you are, your fears, your hurts and your desires, and make a gift to yourself. Live a few hours, half a day or one day of experiencing just being. Open to anything with no exceptions nor prejudices. Without a plan, spend the day in a city and be open to any experience that comes along. Do whatever you feel like doing at the moment, window-shopping, a movie, a meal, a visit to a museum, a cup of coffee, an ice cream cone. Just relax and be. Any thing can happen or nothing. If someone talks to you and you feel like answering do so, if you don't feel like answering then don't. Accept it as it is and observe yourself. Accept yourself as you are. Observe yourself and your feelings during this exercise and after. You should feel refreshed and energized. Repeat the exercise whenever you feel it.

Pretend you are a perfectly healthy beautiful human being. You are free of worries and commitments. Go for a walk alone in the forest or in the mountains. Feel the air on your skin blowing through your hair, listen to the birds if there are any or to the silence, feel the sun if it is shining warm on your skin. Soak it all in and be aware of where you are and what you see. If you live in the city, you can take a walk in the very early hours of the morning while the city is still asleep, make the same experience with seeing, listening and feeling. The result is the same. Awareness of yourself living the moment.

My own favorite way to space out when I feel that I am in a rut or when something is bothering me and I don't know how to handle it. I take time off in the middle of the afternoon and I go to see a movie. I enjoy sitting in an almost empty theatre with a big bag of popcorn and a coke while everyone else is busy working. I feel I am doing something I am not supposed to do and I don't care. So I enjoy it all the more. It is very therapeutic because I take distance from myself, my life, my circumstances, my problems and I come out refreshed.

# 10

# On Dedication

Dedication is, to devote oneself, to employ oneself, to give attention to, to give of oneself. The question is how many of us actually practice that. To give of ourselves, to be totally devoted, give our undivided attention to a project, a cause or a person. I mean how many of us do this selflessly without an ulterior selfish motive. Imagine yourself being dedicated to something totally, giving it your undivided attention, going out of your way and doing your very best. Would there be any doubt in your mind at all that you will be successful in achieving your goal? Of course not, when you are so dedicated, the result is almost guaranteed because you have committed yourself selflessly with one aim and that is to succeed.

Now imagine if each of us were dedicated to make our individual life the best we possibly can, in every way that we can and I am not only talking about material luxuries, which no doubt is nice to have. I am thinking more about our personal qualities and values. Qualities in our personalities which affect our attitude towards life in general, and standards of value by which we live our life, that bring us the invaluable rewards of love, happiness, good health and peace of mind. Attributes and virtues that no amount of money can ever buy. If we each were dedicated to each other, in particular to those closest to us, to see that we can work together, live together and for each other with a common cause and that for the good of all life, would not our world be a better place to live in?

Unfortunately, without delving in to past or present history and ugly details, mankind in general has not exactly been dedicated to making our world, of which we all are an equal part of, a better place to live for everyone and certainly not for our children. The motto for most people is to get whatever you want, whenever you can and however you can. And the more you have, the more you want and this brings you back to square one and you start all over again. This makes me think of a little mouse circling around trying to catch its own tail achieving nothing and going nowhere. Are we not perhaps similar, running round in circles making ourselves dizzy and miserable, trying to achieve the wrong goals, and missing out on the truth and the meaning of life completely? As Robert Frost wrote '*We dance round in a ring and suppose, but the secret sits in the middle and knows.'*

We can choose to change all that by dedicating and committing ourselves to take an active part towards a new world, a better world for us and for the next generations, which can only manifest if we all participate. We can each begin with our own personal life, our own home and family, children and relatives, friends and neighbors, colleagues and business associates and in our town. We can be dedicated to keeping our minds open to communicate, to being flexible, understanding above all tolerant and peace loving, to being open, to change and to growth.

Too many of us willingly fall in to the trap and are very quick to criticize others for their weaknesses; drug addicts, alcoholics, criminals or anyone who does anything that is not to our liking. Instead of judging others concentrate on yourself, stop and look at yourself and watch that you are doing the right thing by setting a good example. You will be achieving more towards a better world and doing yourself a favor if you did this, rather than making a habit of criticizing or blaming others.

Many conveniently blame God for all the miseries of mankind. God is blamed for all the wars, all the natural catastrophes and everything that goes wrong in our personal lives. Some doubt the existence of God. Many usually say 'If there is a God, where is he, why doesn't he do something?' We need to remind ourselves that God gave us, human beings, the greatest gifts of all, intelligence, liberty, freedom of thought and the power of the word and action to do as we please. We are God's most cherished creatures above all others. In our make up we have all the other kingdoms, the mineral, the plant and animal kingdoms. If we choose to refuse to take responsibility for our own senseless actions causing misery for ourselves and for others, then we add insult to injury and we doubt the existence of God, how can we expect God to help us. It is not up to God to put our world right. There is no one up there in heaven sitting on a throne that is going to wave a magic wand to put our life or world in order. We are going to have to do that ourselves.

It is up to us, each one of us, to find the God within us, the love and energy within us and make this work for us and through us for the good of all around us. When mankind is destructive mankind destroys nothing but mankind. Although human beings have been given the gift of intelligence and are considered higher than the mineral, plant and animal kingdom, when human beings are destructive, they actually destroy nothing but themselves for God's nature is far stronger and will ultimately outgrow mankind. Human beings have no control over the kingdom of nature. One only has to think of all the natural catastrophes that have plagued mankind against which human beings are helpless. There are unwritten laws of Nature to be recognized and obeyed. People who work closely with nature are very aware of this. No matter how much we humans fight, how much we destroy, nature will ultimately outlast all of us for many millions of years to come. We humans cannot master nor destroy nature. We can only destroy ourselves. We should look within our Self and reflect on this. The focus should be within.

# 11

# On Detachment

Buddha tells us to practice detachment. Let's look at the meaning of the word detachment. The dictionary says detachment means to be removed, to be separated and disconnected. Now how can I do that, you may ask, to be detached and feel concern, enjoyment or sadness at the same time? The answer is you can, by being independent of that which you have or are doing. When you recognize that everything is passing and nothing is stagnant, even you are passing, you begin to look at and understand the impermanence of everything around you including yourself. You begin to develop a new awareness and a relationship to the world around you. You might be alive and happy today; what makes you so sure it will be the same tomorrow, next week or next month. You might be enjoying perfect health today, but are you absolutely sure you will not fall ill tomorrow? Anyone enjoying the best of health can also fall ill suddenly, have a heart attack, a stroke, develop a tumor, have an accident, get paralyzed. You might have a perfect happy relationship today, are you so sure this will not change tomorrow or the day after? Your partner might fall in love with someone else or worse still die. You have a job today but tomorrow you might get fired. How do you know for sure? I can go on and go on with similar very unpleasant examples just to prove to you the impermanence of life and circumstances.

You just never know do you? All the securities and all the guarantees, all the defenses you surround and protect yourself with can disappear in a moment, for one reason or another, through circumstances beyond your control. You cannot hold on to your health, to love or to life. There is nothing that you can hold on to and keep forever. Absolutely nothing. At the same time impermanence also means the negative situations can turn to a positive. For example, you are terminally ill and then by a miracle you are cured. You are poor one day and the next day you win millions in the lottery or you inherit a fortune from a forgotten uncle or aunt, you are lonely today and then you meet someone special, in one second you fall in love and your whole world changes. You can think of many more happy similar episodes that could change your life overnight for the better. Miracles as well as catastrophes happen every day.

My question to you now is. If you keep this knowledge in mind, how can you be attached to anything? You can certainly be aware of the reality of the moment and you can enjoy it, while you have it, knowing that it is in passing. Realizing that it is in passing and that it will come to an end some time and the moment finally comes when it is over, how can you get upset? The lesson to learn and practice here is never to take anything for granted and the other lesson to learn is that we cannot possess or hold on to anything forever so we need to let go when the time calls for us to let go. We need to learn to do this without regrets or resentments. We need to learn to take the good memories with us, to discard the bad memories and to go on to something new, whatever it is, and to keep on remembering that this too will pass.

Living with detachment for me means that I live the moment very aware of my own attitude towards others. I listen more attentively when I communicate with people and I enjoy every happy moment intensively, because I know it will not continue forever. When a good time is over for me, or I lose some luxuries that I am accustomed to, I do not break down nor does the world come to and end for me. I am still who I am. I am not any different without the artificial trimmings, than when I was with. Who I am no one can touch or take away from me. Living with detachment also helps me to find strength and patience, to suffer through the bad times in my life with dignity, knowing that these bad times too cannot last forever and will eventually pass. Knowing that the sorrow will have an end is like seeing a light at the end of a dark tunnel, and if I keep going concentrating on this light, sooner later I will get there, so I have no reason to despair.

Recognizing, accepting and remembering the fact that absolutely nothing is stagnant in life and all is in constant motion and your world is changing continuously either way, you naturally become detached. You, the Self is independent of all what is going on around you. You observe everything and you enjoy everything if you have a reason to enjoy and you are sad or suffer when things are bad. But the real you is uninvolved and remains untouched, you are making the experience and having the feelings, yes, but you know that situations pass and you will still be there. When you learn to live with this awareness you find yourself detached from feeling such as anger, revenge, hate or resentments. Even pain. You take yourself and life a little less seriously. You can laugh. Actually you will experience that the more you practice detachment the more you will be able to discard negative feelings and develop positive attributes such as understanding, tolerance compassion and love. Practicing detachment makes you the master and not the slave nor the victim of circumstances in your life.

When you first begin to practice detachment, you might find yourself going through a period of a feeling as if you were cut off from all reality and far away from everything, not really involved. This is the other extreme which you need to experience too before you are able to find the real balance. After a while as you keep on practicing and going back and forth with your feelings from being either totally detached or very attached, you will begin to understand the difference and learn to touch that golden middle line. You will be able to find the perfect balance, of how to live your life with awareness and involved but detached.

The idea is to see life as a stage with yourself playing a role and you can observe yourself playing this temporary role with detachment.

# 12

# On Spirituality

There is great interest in esoterics in the western world currently and it is very fashionable to be spiritual. Spiritual poverty is widespread and people are vulnerable and easily influenced either by charlatans who see their opportunity to get rich quickly, or by those who mean well but do not know enough. Both are dangerous and can lead to much harm. It seems to me as if everyone is walking around trying to impress someone else with being spiritual. Experiences are exchanged or discussed in the same way as one would discuss the latest wines or foods in a restaurant, or the latest designer suit. What does being spiritual mean or, how is one spiritual? I have known many who were supposedly religious people and went to church every Sunday, but were not spiritual. At the same time I have known others who never pray in public and are not religious at all, but are in fact very spiritual. Being spiritual does not mean keeping a strict vegetarian diet, nor does it mean floating around on clouds in slow motion with dreamy eyes and in angelic absentminded smile on one's face. Listening to new age space music around the clock, or wearing light color clothing does not mean that one is spiritual, nor is quoting the names of all the gurus you can think of, or reading every new age book that gets published. Lighting incense or candles, meditating, chanting mantras, visiting Ashrams, workshops and seminars without understanding the essence of the teaching, does not make one spiritual either. All these things are fine if the individual does, whatever is done, naturally and experiences inner growth and transformation intimately. If, however, it is imitated, forced or faked, or done out of curiosity or for not having anything better to do, all of the above become nothing but artificial trappings, done merely for show, to impress and to convince oneself and/or others of one's spirituality.

The fact is we are all by nature spiritual beings. The difference is only that some of us are more in touch with our spirituality than others are. Being spiritual actually is a very intimate personal feeling that has nothing to do with all of the above. Spirituality is very sensuous, it is being very aware of your senses and difficult to be defined in simple words. As a rule genuinely spiritual people do not talk about being spiritual they just simply are, with every breath they breathe and with their senses every moment of their life. They live in close touch with the miracle of life with every breath. They appreciate life and accept everything that it brings, all the pleasures and all the sufferings, they know love, beauty, compassion, submission and humility. Spirituality is lived and integrated in their daily lives naturally, no matter where they are or what they happen to be occupied with. It is nothing that one thinks about. It is living truth and simplicity and being constantly aware of being a part of a Higher Power, the Source.

It is your choice what method you want to try out to make your own experiences, what might be good for one can be wrong for the other. No one can advise you on what is best for you. Only you can know that and the best way to come to this knowledge is by understanding yourself and what you need. You can do whatever your heart desires, but be critical of what you choose to do and how you allow yourself to be guided and by whom. The path is long and is bound to present you with many difficulties that you will have to overcome yourself. How you choose to overcome these difficulties determines your progress. Do not be tempted to take shortcuts because there are no shortcuts to take. You should be careful of anyone who tries to convince you otherwise. There is no such thing as 'fast food' spirituality. No workshop can offer you enlightenment or nirvana within a week no matter how good it is. It might help you one step further, yes, but certainly not more. Any sect, Guru or group that demand that you obey blindly, robbing you of your freedom to think and freedom to move, should be avoided like poison. Any group that claims absolute knowledge or is secretive about its activities should be likewise avoided. Most certainly avoid those who claim unrealistic high prices or con you to giving huge donations in return for salvation, also those who demand that you take distance from family, friends or society and give up your life for their cause becoming totally dependent on them. Seek those who are willing to guide you and help you but who at the same time encourage you to stand on your own feet, to be free and independent.

Spiritually active people are in every field and on every level, occupied with constructive activities. They look and behave as normal as everyone else and are always very active. The characteristics of genuine spiritual people are: Serenity, inner strength, compassion, love, intuition, warmth, joy, understanding, tolerance, self confidence and a sense of deep inner peace.

They have no need to display their spirituality to the public, nor do they attempt to convince or impress anyone. They just are as they are quite natural and quite reachable.

# 13

# On Humor

It is said that having a sense of humor is a grace from God. I personally believe that. I believe that God has a great sense of humor and sometimes I also think that God likes to play jokes on us human beings! If you really observe your life and that of others, you have to admit there is a lot of funny stuff going on all the time. You just have to see it that way. Having the ability to see the funny side of things and to be able to laugh at the world and oneself included is an art. It is definitely an asset and adds a lot more fun into your life. I was always known to my family and friends, as looking on at the world through rose colored glasses. 'When are you going to grow up and take off those rose colored glasses of yours?' They would say to me. My sense of humor and ability to laugh easily, for them, was looking at the world with childish eyes and unrealistic. It never bothered me, the important point for me is that I can laugh. That is the medicine that keeps me carefree, youthful and healthy. True, some people are born with this natural gift but one can learn it too the same as one can learn anything else. Work on it, try to develop a sense of humor, try to see the funny side of things. There is always a funny side even in the most serious situations. Smile at the world as much as you can. Try to acquire lightness and easiness in your way of dealing with yourself and your world. As a matter of fact when you work on yourself to be open, flexible, compassionate and forgiving, the lightness of being will automatically follow. It is far from being childish or being irresponsible and it does not mean laughing at others either. On the contrary it is being in close touch with all the facets of the intimacies of life, understanding life and being natural and compassionate towards all beings.

There is a child in each of us that we need not bury when we are adults. Most of us adults, unfortunately, tend to leave this child aspect behind, as we grow older, in the belief that being adult means being serious. Truth is, it is possible and also spiritual, to be both very serious and have the ability, to be carefree, to have fun and laugh, at the same time. A well balanced person, self-confident with an inner peace, thinks nothing of behaving or enjoying life like a child. Be natural, childlike and simple without being childish. See the humor in the fact that no matter who we are, we all come from the same source in the same way and we will all end in the same way whether we are mummified or not! We are all subject to the wide spectrum of feelings from pure ecstasy to deep depression regardless of who we are. Love, joy and a sense of humor, the greatest gifts of all, are free of charge, with an invisible sign that says 'Help yourself, take all you want. There's more than enough to go round for everyone.' It is also a well-known fact that laughter is the best natural cure for many illnesses and in particular for cancer. It has been proven scientifically that laughter produces juices in the body that heal.

In closing keep in mind always that it is love and joy that are the motor of life. No matter what happens to you or to your world, if you live with love and joy in your heart, compassion and forgiveness for yourself, your fellow beings and nature around you, you cannot possibly go wrong. Remember always to shun fear, doubt and despair no matter how tough it might get, for they are your worst enemies. Think of Sindbad the sailor and the fun he had, in between his adventures, killing his monsters. Look out for your monsters that creep up on you in the form of resentments, laziness, insecurities or depression, draw out your swords of energy, courage and belief and get those monsters before they get you. Keep them in check and always under control.

Hopefully this book will inspire you to make an effort to change your life for the better. To keep your motivation going it helps to acquire a habit of reading something on self-improvement every day, even if it is for fifteen minutes only. This will be the fuel that will keep you going. Many self help books you can read again and again. This book on change can serve you well if you keep it handy and refer to it whenever you feel you need a gentle reminder to stay on the right track.

I wish you much love in your heart and joy in your life, lightness of being and much fun and laughter on your journey. Remember you are never alone. We are all together on the same temporary journey of life. The more compassion, empathy and understanding we have towards each other the easier and the more pleasurable our journey will be.

*The most lost day of all is the day
on which we do not laugh*

*Nicholas Chamfort*

# 14

# Self Assessment Exercises

Answer the following comments now and check back in a few weeks, months or years, to see whether and how you have made any progress.

## *ASSESSMENT 1*

Which of the following comments do you say?

Sometimes / rarely / often / never

UUUgh I hate to get up in the morning

I am too old/too young

I am toot fat/ too thin

I am not good enough

I worry about this or that

I feel guilty

I get irritated over many things

I get angry/I have a temper

I am too tall/too short

I feel sorry for myself

I blame myself for

I am no-one special

I hate to go to work

I hate myself

I hate my life

I hate others

I am just a housewife

I am jealous of

I hate to be alone

I cannot be alone

I wish I were like

If only I had done this or that,
then maybe…..

I blame others

If you catch yourself stating negative statements, write them down, and make a promise to yourself to change this, observe and train yourself to change. Check back with this list every now and again and control your speech, your thought pattern and your behavior. Above all, be honest with yourself! Try to eliminate negative dialogue in your head. Replace it with 'I love to....'

## ASSESSMENT 2

Take your time and answer the following question honestly, regardless of what your present circumstances are. Do not worry whether what you want to do is useful or not. Try not to limit your thoughts while answering. The goal is for you to get in touch with your innermost feelings by answering spontaneously and freely.

Three things that **I do best**.

1.
2.
3.

Three things that **I love most to do**.

1.
2.
3.

Three things that **make me happy**

1.
2.
3.

## *ASSESSMENT 3*

Six things that make me feel bad, guilty, afraid, worried, angry and resentful. Be honest, no one is going to read this but you. Then analyze your feeling and ask yourself why you feel this way. Work on changing your attitude from negative to positive.

1.

2.

3.

4.

5.

6.

## ASSESSMENT 4

Make a list of outstanding good work experiences that you have had, whether recognized or not, paid or not, such as volunteer work, at social parties, holidays, school, work, meeting someone, both private and professional. What did you learn about yourself from those good experiences you have had? Feel free to use separate sheets of paper.

## ASSESSMENT 5

Do this exercise in writing.

- If you could change your life now, how would you like to have it different? To get to know the real you, you must be honest with yourself.

- What is stopping you?

- List what steps you can begin to take right now to change.

*Margo Kirtikar Ph.D*

# Recommended Reading and Studies

- Alice A. Bailey, 'Esoteric Psychology,' Vol. 1, Lucis Publishing Co., London, 1991.
- J.G. Bennett, 'Intimation' Beshara publications, 1975.
- H.P.Blavatsky, 'From the Caves and Jungles of Hindostan.' The Theosophical Publishing House, Madras, 1983.
- Louis Charpentier 'The Mysteries of Chartres Cathedral.' Thorsons Publishing Group Ltd., Wellinborough, Nprthhampshire, 1988.
- Lin Cochran, 'Secrets of the Universe,' Warner Books, Inc. 1989.
- Shakti Gawain, 'Living in the Light,' Whatever Publishing Inc., San Rafael, CA. 1986.
- Louise L.Hay, 'You can HealYour Life.' Hay House, Santa Monica, CA. 1984.
- Napoleon Hill, 'Think and Grow Rich,' Hawthorn Bppks Inc., NYC.1966.
- J. Krishnamurti, 'Krishnamurti's Notebook,' Harper and Row, London 1976.
- Peter Mandel, 'Esogetics,' Energetik Verlag Gmbh, Sulzbach, Taunus, 1993.
- C.S. Nott, 'Further Teachings of Gurdjeff,' Samuel Weiser Inc., York Beach, Maine, 1984.

- P.D. Ouspensky, 'In Search if the Miraculous,' Harcourt Brace Jovanovich, N.Y. 1977.
- M. Scott Peck, M.D. 'The Road Less Traveled,' Simon & Scguster, NYC, 1978.
- Shastri, Hari Prasad, 'Direct Experience of Reality,' Shanti Sadan, London, 1975.
- Geshe Rabten, 'The Mind and its Function,' Editions Rabten Choeling. Le Mont Pelerin, 1992.
- Shankara, 'Interpretation of the Upanishads,' S.N. Publications, Delhi, 1988.
- Idries Shah, 'The Sufis,' Doubleday, NY 1964.
- The Upanishads, Penguin 1981.
- Swami Vishnu Devananda, 'Meditation and Mantras,' OM Lotus Publishing Co. NYC 1978.

## *Negative and Positive Energies*

| Negative | Positive |
|---|---|
| *to minimize* | *to maximize* |
| Anger | Acceptance |
| Absentmindedness | Awareness |
| Anxiety | Calmness |
| Boredom | Communication |
| Criticism | Common sense |
| Defeat | Compassion |
| Depression | Concentration |
| Doubt | Confidence |
| Envy | Courage |
| Fear | Decision |
| Forgetfulness | Detachment |
| Gossip | Determination |
| Greed | Discipline |
| Guilt | Enthusiasm |
| Hate | Faith |
| Hysteria | Forgiveness |
| Ignorance | Generosity |
| Ill Health | Good Health |
| Indecision | Gratefulness |
| Insecurity | Harmony |
| Jealousy | Intelligence |
| Laziness | Joy |
| Limitations | Knowledge |
| Rebellion | Laughter |

| | |
|---|---|
| Resentment | Love |
| Resistance | Motivation |
| Scattered | Openness |
| Stagnation | Order |
| Stupidity | Tolerance |
| Worry | Understanding |

*The energy we have at our disposal is neutral and therefore, can be used by us either way, constructive or destructive. The choice is ours. It is to our own advantage and general well being, to maximize the positive energies in us by exercising and practicing the positive character traits and to keep under control all the negative energies.*

# *Change*

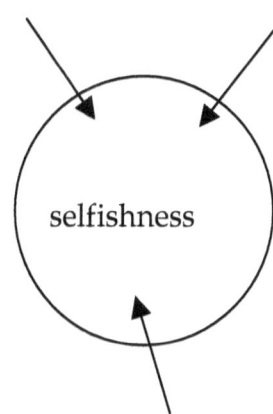

from the
**past world**
of selfishness

to the
**future world**
of altruism

| | | | | |
|---|---|---|---|---|
| **C** | Corruption | **C** | Compassion |
| **H** | Hostility | **H** | Harmony |
| **A** | Avoidance | **A** | Awareness |
| **N** | Narrowness | **N** | Nature |
| **G** | Greed | **G** | Goodwill |
| **E** | Egotism | **E** | Enthusiasm |

# About the Author

 Margo who was born and raised in Baghdad, was educated in Arab, French, British, Swiss and American Schools. She experienced several extreme personal and cultural changes in her life. At the end of her teenage years the family, because of a civil war in Baghdad, moved to London. Two years later she married a Swiss, moved to Switzerland where she gave birth to her three daughters. While adapting to the Swiss life, marriage, and children, she embarked in her mid-twenties on a business career. In her mid-thirties she moved with her children to the United States where she spent the next fourteen years.

In Manhattan she continued to be active in the international business world and soon she joined the adult student force and continued with her education attending university. She completed degrees in International Economics, International Banking, in Psychology including a doctorate in Metaphysics. In 1990 she left New York and returned to Switzerland.

Being of Syrian/Indian origin and growing up in the Arab Christian/Moslem/Jewish culture of Baghdad and Damascus, plus the influence of the Indian Hindu culture through her father, it is not surprising that the metaphysical world and spirituality have always been a very real, natural and integrated part of Margo's daily life. She is also an avid student of religions and believes strongly that all major religions bring us the same important message in different forms and languages.

Margo also believes in continued adult education and she is convinced that the source of her limitless energy, youthfulness and good health is her active, constructive and creative life style. The first self-transformation she was aware of was when she moved from the Eastern to the Western culture. The second major painful transformation she experienced was at the end of her fourteen years of marriage. It was in New York when she was in her forties, that Margo, who is also an accomplished artist, experienced yet another major transformation in her being. This manifested in her artwork changing from impressionism to abstract art overnight. Art and painting is food and exercise for her soul. The acquisition of book knowledge and writing is her mental food and exercise and these are just as important as the food and exercise for her physical body. Margo currently counsels, lectures, holds workshops on spiritual development.

Margo likes to quote a Sufi Master called Hujwiri who wrote:

> *'there are three forms of culture:*
> *worldly culture,*
> *the mere acquisition of information;*
> *religious culture,*
> *following rules;*
> *and the elite culture –*
> *Self Development.'*

Contact:

Margo Kirtikar Ph.D.
Seefeldstrasse 34
8008 Zurich
Switzerland
email: margo@visionsunusual.com
www.visionsunusual.com